22 Steps to the Light of Your Soul

Embrosewyn Tazkuvel

OTHER CAPTIVATING, THOUGHT-PROVOKING BOOKS
by Embrosewyn Tazkuvel

Secret Earth Series
LABYRINTH OF IMMORTALITY *(Book 1)*

Psychic Awakening Series
CLAIRVOYANCE *(Book 1)*
TELEKINESIS *(Book 2)*
DREAMS *(Book 3)*

AURAS
How To See, Feel And Know

UNLEASH YOUR PSYCHIC POWERS

PSYCHIC SELF DEFENSE

LOVE YOURSELF
Secret Key To Transforming Your Life

Oracles of Celestine Light Trilogy
GENESIS *(First Book of Light)*
NEXUS *(Second Book of Light)*
VIVUS *(Third Book of Light)*

Dedicated to
my wife Sumara;
my inspiration and fulfillment
and to the children of light in our lives:
Lyndi, Shaina, Tairel, Anya, Kristelle, Kayla & Angel

I love you each with all my heart.
Thank you for teaching me so much and for sharing some of
your life with me.

Published by Kaleidoscope Productions
1467 Siskiyou Boulevard, #9; Ashland, OR 97520
www.kaleidoscope-publications.com

Cover design and book layout by Sumara Elan Love
www.3wizardz.com

ISBN 978-0-938001-19-5

TABLE OF CONTENTS

~PROLOGUE~

December 22, 1995

Alone, in the fading darkness, I sit in my despair, my head buried in my hands, tepid tears seeping down my warm, flush cheeks. For three long and painful months I have wrestled with an unsolvable riddle. The answer lies beyond the dawns mist. Like a cool wind that rustles through crisp, autumn leaves, I can sense it; I reach for it, desperate for solace, but the wraith of promise slips through my fingers evermore.

At last, when my final shred of pride has been abashed, when the walls around my heart have swayed and crumbled into dust, I have the humility **to ask**…to ask for something higher, greater than my simple body and exhausted mind, to intervene, to lift a distant lamp, to light a path for me, to illuminate me with an answer beyond my knowing.

Like whispers of echoes reverberating in a distant canyon far and unseen, comes an evocative voice, hauntingly surreal, piercing me to my core, endowing me with answers of enlightenment my mind did not fathom, drenching me with knowledge that basks my parched soul in joy. The long night gives birth to a dawn of a thousand lights and in fulfillment and humble astonishment I realize that I have opened the transcendent luminescence of my soul. In humility, I simply sought an answer, but now my restless mind is aswirl with questions. Thus begins a wondrous journey of discovery…

September 22, 2004

This is a book for the children of my heart, that they may have a guide to finding the sweetness and savor of life, and always have a part of me with them. If others can find hope, inspiration and benefit from these words as well, we all share joy.

~INTRODUCTION~

June 2010

I n my journey of personal and spiritual expansion, I learned we each have a higher part of us that calls us to the greatness we can be. My search to discover the greater light led to this book.

I make mistakes like anyone else, and am often challenged by quandaries to which I cannot fathom a good answer. As I opened up to the greater enlightenment, it was as if my soul, my spiritual essence, took wing and went to some glorious far off place returning with marvelous answers I would have never conceived. The messenger that brought back the answers and dropped them in my mind and imagination was someone who seemed very different than me and remotely distant while also intricately a part. How great was my joy when realized I was discovering my own best friend, my higher, spiritual self, the essence of the light of my soul- Embrosewyn Tazkuvel.

I first experienced the revelations of the *22 Steps to the Light of Your Soul* back in December of 1995 as I mentioned in the Prologue. In 2004 I wrote down the 22 steps in Embrosewyn's poetic style, hoping they would linger in the memory of my children and anyone else who might read them. Instead of publishing the 22 steps at that time, I decided to incorporate them into a novel, hoping an engaging story would motivate more people to read and benefit from them. However, in 2005, through Embrosewyn my higher self, I was called upon to begin revelating and transcribing the *Oracles of Celestine Light*, which has just recently been published, all 807 pages.

The Oracles had been an all-consuming endeavor for 5 years.

With its completion I looked to jump into a long list of other writing projects that had been neglected during the previous five years. One of those, and an important one, was the 22 Steps to the Light of Your Soul. Contemplating the storyline of the novel, I realized it could be sometime before it was completed and ready for publication. In the meantime, sitting unpublished on my computer, nobody was benefiting from the marvelous insights for life presented in the 22 steps.

I resolved not to wait any longer when I already had a completed manuscript, but to publish the 22 steps now, independent and unincorporated into a novel and to finish the novel at some other time in the future. Certainly that seems backwards of the way sequels and spinoffs are usually done in the publishing world, but just as certainly, it is the right thing to do.

Though the steps begin with 1 and end with 22 there is a peculiar non-sequential order to them. The first chapter is actually both the first and the last chapter- Chapter 22. It is completely unlike any of the other chapters in both style and substance. You should read it before all others and complete your reading of the 22 Steps with this chapter as well. It is the Alpha and the Omega, both the beginning and the end. It gives more meaning to everything else in the book. The remaining chapters should be read in the order of the subjects that most draw your interest. These are the areas you are most receptive for accelerated personal growth in right now. The particular order in which you master them is up to you and your personal needs and circumstances. But you'll soon discover that each step you understand and incorporate into your persona and character will reward you with more fulfillment and joy in life; more than you can imagine.

May you grow in your light reading the 22 Steps to the Light of Your Soul as much as I did receiving and writing them.

Namaste,

~Embrosewyn Tazkuvel

The 1st Step

THE PURPOSE OF LIFE

I've wandered in a daze beset by unfathomable questions. Who are we? Why are we here? Surely life has a grander purpose than is obvious in day to day existence? Is this life it? Is death the last hurrah or is there more beyond?

And my soul took flight and returned with an answer...

When the universe was birthed in fire and majesty, when the wind of creation filled all of space, your ancient soul dwelt even then among the endless stars. The cradle of your birth is but a gossamer dream passing you from the glory you have known to the brilliance you shall become. You are a twinkling star that has illuminated the sky, flown now from the heavens to light the world.

You were not born by idle chance nor intended to walk the Earth in forgotten trepidacious steps. Your life has a greater purpose than simply living, a grander promise than mere relaxation upon the morrow. Abiding within your essence are wonderful talents and abilities that uniquely proclaim your name. Seek earnestly to develop the alluring pursuits that beckon to you; resonant endeavors which compel your enduring interest, passion, pleasure and excellence. Upon their wings you will soar and in the purposeful expansion of your divine endowments you shall discover a sweetness of life that ever abides.

You journey on a sacred quest of the soul, a timeless odyssey of self discovery. With quiet reverence and barely bridled anticipation, do not hesitate to deeply explore the luminous labyrinths of your inner self. Far within the darkest recess of your most secret place, where only the brave heart will venture, is the sacred Mirror of Illumination, solitary in a fog. Gaze closely, without deceit, upon your quavering visage to honestly see who you are today. Smile upon your virtues and cry upon your flaws, then with courage twice as great, reach through the tenuous tendrils of misting contradictions to see your soul of light and glory. For in the illumination from that glorious light, you see not only who you are, but also who you can become and until you truly know yourself, you can never take your power nor find your destiny.

The path of life before you is fraught with shadowy dangers and perilous pitfalls, joyous heights, heinous betrayals and unbreakable bonds of kinship and love. Each step, bold or timid, forward or backward, shall be a school. Each challenge, momentous or miniscule, successful or naught shall move you closer to your goal. From lessons learned you either pass the test or gain the knowledge to succeed when it comes again. Therefore, embrace and give thanks for the humbling shells of your bitter defeats and heart-wrenching failures; for within them are the seeds of tomorrow's victories.

Whether life's darker moments tear you down or build you up depends upon your perception of the dance of life. Choose to learn and grow from every experience; even those that weary your spirit and abase your pride. Even when painfully pushed down, you can rise again from the ashes, reborn with renewed purpose, blessed with a clearer insight and swathed in a quiet humility that could have been gained no other way. The path before you will be more lucid now. Life's travails open the depths of your heart to that which has eternal value and unmask the charade of the valueless, banishing it as the dust, to blow away upon the winds of time without worth or memory.

Who you are this moment in time is merely the sum of who you have been, the character you have melded in the furnace of life, created not from your victories or defeats, but from the choices you have made.

Who you will be tomorrow is unwritten. If you have not fully been the light that is your birthright, it is never too late to begin a new page. The book of your life can only be inscribed by your own hand and it is limitless in what you can write and extol upon it.

To fulfill your quest you must fulfill your glory. Take the rough-hewed marble that is your life and chisel and polish a work of wonder that bears your name. This is your legacy and your promise of eternity. If simple rock can be quarried from the Earth and shaped and formed into a work of exquisite art and beauty, how much greater still can you, the master sculptor of your destiny, do with the marbled stone that is your life?

When choices are to be made, consider them well; choose that which has true significance. You do not know the number of the days in your life; therefore, cherish each one as a precious gift, that the last, whenever it will be, shall be your greatest memorial.

Neither gold, nor diamonds, nor the fortunes of Kings shall pass with you upon the sunset of your Earthly sojourn. Eternity's treasures are earned by your actions and your love. Your gold is the nobility of your character. Your luminous ruby is the enduring love of your life's companion. Your precious emeralds are your children of light who know the paths to greatness and fulfillment because you showed them the way.

As you journey through life be mindful of your legacy. After your body has long turned to dust, what will remain from the dynamic essence of your life to benefit and uplift the generations that follow? Though your years may be finite upon the Earth, the grand purpose of life is to invest it in relationships, accomplishments and actions that will endure beyond it. In so doing, the enrichment of your life continues to pour forth a radiant blessing upon the world. Therefore, may your deeds be chosen wisely, creating repercussions that reverberate and flourish beyond your years that your light of love and consideration may continue to shine evermore, inspiring generations yet unborn.

When your journey nears the gates of truth and light that you have sought all of your life, fear not the last sleep. If you have joyously lived life, death will hold no mystery for you. Your eyes shall shine anew and your heart shall beat once more upon a new dawn.

Life and death are two sides of the same face. Death is but a cycle of life, as life is a sequence of death; like the day kisses the night, so too the night once again embraces the day.

If you have fulfilled your promises, they will fulfill you.

If you have lived the life, it will never leave you. You shall dance upon the mountain tops as the sun bursts in warmth and light upon a new day. And the treasures you cherished in life, those that endure through time and space, through eternity and beyond, shall be with you still as the new day begins.

The 2nd Step

WHAT OF BALANCE?

There are so many aspects to living life, so many enticements pulling me this way and that, so many things to consider for personal growth. How do I achieve a good balance of my time, pursuits, traits and beliefs to best maximize my growth?

And my soul took flight and returned with an answer...

The journey of life is like the formidable challenge of fording a mighty river. Swift and furious rush the turbulent waters; pushing, pulling, surprising with bursting waves of cold, unexpected fury. Only with vigilant attention, carefully treading along the unseen conduit of a narrow, passable ford, cautiously balancing upon every small, rounded and slippery rock beneath the restless waters may the bounty and peace of the beautiful, faraway shore be safely reached.

Balance and the renewing cycles of life created from the harmony of its sweet song, is the firm foundation of the universe upon which all things exist. The smallest atom hears its voice. Every planet circling a star dances to its music.

All who cultivate balance find peace and harmony, but whosoever turns their face from balance embraces struggle, and all that forsake balance entirely will wither in a morass of self-destructive actions and bitter frustration.

Yet, from whence does balance spring forth? Only in the

timbre of difference can the harmony of balance be born and only in blended, resonant variation can the symphony of balance play on. A great secret of the ages is that every note has its opposite, as does each aspect of the life that bears your name. Sounded alone they are forlorn and empty but played together in balance they stir the heart and uplift the soul.

Consider the orbit of the Moon about the Earth. How is it that the Moon neither falls into the Earth nor spins away into space leaving the planet abandoned and alone? By balance alone it remains. The momentum of the Moon as it revolves about the Earth would sling it away into the abyss of space, if the opposing gravity of the Earth did not irresistibly tug upon it creating a balance which holds it in orbit. The same balance of opposing energies is played by the Earth promenading around the sun, even as the sun circles around the center of the galaxy. Balance sets the table of stability for growth and harmony to flourish.

Balance does not mean equal but rather equilibrium. Especially when multiple aspects require time, energy or resources, the equilibrium between the many creates a beneficial balance based not upon equality, but need. If a man has a beautiful meadow of flourishing, green grass but some acres are kissed more by the sun, others more by the shade, while a third area dips its roots into more fertile ground, he cannot treat all parts equally. The ideal amount of water for the shady section would be too meager for that which lies in the sun and it would wither and dry. If adequate water is given to the sunny patch it would be excessive for the shady portion, rotting the roots and stunting the grass. The fertile piece requires no added nutrients for the grass to grow tall and lush, but without additional nutrients the other parcels will be underdeveloped and pale. Only by giving each part of the whole that which it needs, some more water or nutrition, others less, will the entire meadow be blessed with verdant, green lushness and abundant life.

Consider your orbit within the galaxy of your life. Where is your balance, both within and without, and from whence does it come? Does your mind, your heart, your body and your spirit have an equilibrium that supports personal growth, loving relationships, vibrant health and delightful happiness? Are you well rounded in your disposition and character? Do you equitably balance and divide your finite time among work, play, exercise, education and relationships of love, family and friends? Or are some things gluttons, living beyond their balance, infringing upon the time and needs of the others, robbing them of sustenance and destabilizing your intrepid ship of life?

Within all things dwells a compelling attraction to its needs, as within all people there is a yearning to fill the empty places and achieve balance. Too often that which would give balance and be advantageous is labeled as evil and shunned rather than recognized as a necessary but neglected part of the whole. What is evil but good that is out of balance, either overindulging in that which is beneficial in moderation, or seeking to quench an unfilled thirst or hunger in dark places because the cupboard within is bare or inadequate?

An out-of-balance person is at war with himself, pitting desire against principles, passion against reason and appetite against judgment. Like a sailing ship on a great voyage of discovery, all parts of the vessel are necessary to complete the journey. Sails without a mast are as little use as a compass never viewed. If a rivalry exists within you, it is your soul crying for balance and if you do not heed its plea you are doomed to shed acrid tears of sorrow and frustration all of your days.

Your worthy goals and desires must be soundly anchored upon the rock of virtuous principles. The two united create a synergistic amplification, unveiling possibilities that would have remained hidden to solitary discovery. For desires alone are like bees flitting from one flower to another without fulfillment, and principles alone are like a man who refuses to eat at a feast because the tablecloth is unsatisfactory.

So too, the fire of your passions must be balanced with the steadfastness of your sound reasoning. For reason, standing alone, confines you to a cage and passion, unattended, leads to great errors and makes a buffoon of those who might otherwise be saints.

Your appetite for the bounties of life must be weighed with your wise judgment as to their true benefit. For appetite alone can become a furnace that burns you until consumed, or produces a useless and pitiful shell of a life; while judgment alone sours one so thoroughly that even looking in a mirror is a displeasure.

Embrace all of your being with love and joy. Give each element proper attention, merging your many aspects into a rhythmic resonance that your whole life may be balanced and expansive. Thus, discord will be quieted and a sweet melody of peace and harmony will pervade your soul, ever singing a song of oneness that soothes your troubles and invigorate your life.

The 3rd Step

WHAT OF CHARACTER?

I try to be a good person but I know I've made mistakes and hurt people I care about. How can I more fully live my best qualities?

And my soul took flight and returned with an answer...

The steadfast nobility of your character is the robust rock upon which you build the incomparable temple of your life. Whether your life becomes a towering edifice, awed and respected, or a crumbling ruin destroyed by a weak foundation of vacillating, self-centered principles, is decided by every choice you make. Your character is not a birthright but a chosen path. It is the manifestation of your secret inner thoughts, motivations, judgments and opinions into standards of conduct and parameters of action that define your life and legacy. Ultimately your character is an inescapable reflection of your own self worth. It is either a noble inner light, or a petty, unworthy darkness and you must decide each day and with every action, which it shall be.

It matters not how high you have risen in the tempestuous world, but only how far you have soared inside the quintessence of your inner nobility, for character has no connection to wealth, education or social position. The character you weave into your soul becomes the very essence of your eternal life force and does not fade into mist when the body turns to dust. Long after you have passed from the Earth, the permeating energy of the character you exhibited, for better or worse, will linger and influence everyone whose life you touched.

Character is an evolving work built upon a foundation of proven and cherished principles and expanded by an open-minded desire to ever be improving. This you may have been today, but you can be someone greater tomorrow. You are not perfect, nor shall ever be, but continually striving to more fully embody and express higher ideals and worthy personal traits should be an ongoing pursuit. Be like a mighty oak; its vast canopy of expansive green leafed branches are ever open to the sky that it may receive beneficial enrichment from the light of all the world. But it also stands upright upon a mighty trunk of indomitable strength that will not bend to the furied force of contrary winds, which may pummel and rage about it for a time, but inevitably will quietly dissolve in a whimpered whisper of defeat.

So too, there will be many alluring and seducing winds that will promise wonder if you will simply abandon your principles for a time. Be wary and steadfast against seducing enticements which invite you to ignore ethos you know to be right. Though their beckoning allure may be tempting, their substance will be revealed to be hollow and empty of fulfillment. Like a stalwart oak, may the roots of an exemplary character be sunk deep into the immutable foundations of your life; that they may ever nourish you with a worthy and noble vision whenever you are faced with a choice of action or deed.

Though walking a higher path may be challenging, knowing the path is always plain. For it is a divine gift of the eternal human spirit to ever know right from wrong. There resides within every mind and resonates within every heart, a connection to an inner voice echoing from the distant stars, softly pricking the conscious and ever so subtly reminding one of the worthiness or unworthiness of every contemplated action or utterance. Though poor choices are often rationalized by vexing circumstances or self-absolved by proclaimed ignorance or insignificance of the error, there is always a moment, however fleeting, when your higher self speaks plainly, and honestly of the truth. Thereby knowing the right, can there ever be justification for committing the wrong?

True nobility of character impels a soul-searching desire to make amends for past mistakes and henceforth walk a higher path in life. Your careless choices of yesterday need not be a weighty millstone forever around your neck, relentlessly trapping you in an ever twirling whirlpool of past mistakes. Only by severing the sinewed rope that unrelentingly holds the sordid stone of yesterday's mistakes can the brilliant sun of tomorrow's promise fully shine. Repentance is the knife that severs the rope, freeing the repentant from the prison of their making. Recognize that you have erred, feel sorry for your mistakes and admit them honestly to those you have wronged. As much as possible make restitution for harm done and humbly ask their forgiveness, vowing to forsake your hurtful shortcomings of the past. Then fulfill your vow. Accomplish these steps and you also can forgive yourself, banish guilt, and set your spirit free to soar to new heights unencumbered by the ponderous weight of past shortcomings. Your past is energetically erased by the meaningful repentance of your heart manifested by the tangible renewal of your actions.

As you are lifted free from the onerous weight of your past misdeeds, remember to extend the same solace of forgiveness to those who may have wronged you in the past, but have asked your forgiveness and exhibited qualities of a sincere repentance for their errors. To completely pardon someone who is honestly sorry for their past mistakes and willing to make amends, is a distinctive mark of the sincerity of your intent to earnestly improve the quality of your own character. Forgiveness discards the poisonous baggage of the past, helps you to become better than you were, and infuses you with an ecstasy of goodness that unchains your tattered heart that it may again sing ebullient songs of joy.

Amongst all the world's virtues, how shall you know the ones that will beneficially lift you up and infuse your character with desirable traits that will uniquely resonate within your heart, mind and soul? When faced with a choice of action or deed, by what standard will you know to choose the right? The answer is so pure and simple that it has been told and retold for countless ages, throughout all generations; a basic foundation of religions and philosophies across the world. In its brevity, it extols an enormous truth, known as The Golden Rule: "**Do unto others as you would have them do unto you.**" By incorporating this simple phrase into every aspect of your life, you will have a gleaming guidepost that will never fail to direct you upon worthy paths that, though sometimes difficult, will always lift you to new heights of self-esteem and nobility, ever challenging you to become more than you were. Though others may sometimes deride your valorous choices, your steadfast conviction and example will not be forgotten. Someday, someone will catch a vision from you and choose to walk a higher path because you were courageous enough to show them the way.

How you treat others; the politeness, attention, respect, courtesy, care and praise you give to them, especially to those of lesser position or social standing, is one of the surest indicators of the nobleness of the character that resides within the shinning star that is your life. Always remember that to, "do unto others as you would have them do unto you" means all others, without discrimination or disdain. As you treat your fellow travelers in the sojourn of life, in grateful reciprocation will they be inclined to so treat you. Nor is there any life without worth, or any person who cannot impart valuable lessons to teach and benefit you, if you will but give them a moment of your focused attention to reveal their glory.

Earnest reciprocation for a kindness that has been received is a hallmark of a person of distinguished character. When someone blesses you with benefit or comfort, you incur an energetic responsibility to reciprocate in some way that brings them equal benefit and comfort. This is a wonderful debt to repay that brings personal growth and expansion to both the giver and the receiver. In truth, reciprocation should be an ever reverberating harmonic energy, continually benefiting those participating in the ongoing energy exchange.

There are occasions when it becomes impossible to reciprocate directly to the generous person who bestowed a kindness upon you, as when a passing stranger gives aid to a stranded traveler. These become special opportunities to begin a reciprocation chain that can continue for unseen generations with profound repercussions that may affect countless people. It is reciprocation by proxy. When you are gifted with assistance and unable to respond directly to the considerate person that aided you, look for opportunities where you can help a distressed stranger in their hour of need even as you were helped in yours. If they offer to repay you in any way, politely decline and explain how you were once assisted by a benevolent benefactor even as you are now helping them. Invite them to continue the reciprocating chain of good energy by giving aid and kindness to a stranger they will surely find in need one day.

If you wish to further expand the energy of reciprocation and thus enlarge your own virtue, consider how you can multiply the good that has been done for you many times again, by being ever ready and willing to generously give compassion, kindness and assistance to both loved ones and strangers as opportunities are presented. Remember too, your own inescapable mortality and do not procrastinate the good that you can do today, for you know not the number of your days on Earth and tomorrow may be too late.

In your travels and search for dynamic growth and enlightenment, be ever willing to labor both physically and mentally. Work is not menial, but empowering, and the reward is not just in the satisfied completion of the task, but also in priceless gems of character bestowed upon you with each step of the enterprise. The foremost compensation for industrious efforts is not what you receive at the end, but what you become in the process.

Invest wisely in your eternity. Your worldly success and material accumulations will not travel with you when you pass this life, but your character endures to ever light your star with radiant sparkle in the endless sky.

May your sterling character ever grow in stature with each day that passes till it has become as inseparable from you as your faithful shadow. When a challenge to virtue or fairness is thrown as a caustic gauntlet before you, may you ever have the abiding courage to do what you know to be right, despite the tawdry controversy or virulent uproar that may ensue.

When others wander in pain in the murky, black nights of their life, may you have the gentle compassion to help and the essential wisdom to guide them to paths of luminous light and a greater hope for the sunrise of tomorrow. Remember, you are not a languid, desert island awash in an empty ocean, but a precious drop in the sparkling sea of life itself, vibrantly connected to all that exists and gently touching the many diverse shores. Know that when you help others to reach their aspirations and dreams or find hope or meaning in their life, you are also lifting yourself and walking the only path to true greatness and nobility.

The fullness of your true character is revealed each day, to you and others in every action you take and every word you say. It is the matchless masterpiece of your soul painted on the glimmering, rainbow canvas of your life. May it ever reveal the greatness and goodness that resides within your valiant heart.

The 4th Step

WHAT OF HABITS?

It is somewhat frustrating when there are things such as a more prudent diet and regular exercise that I know are important for the quality of my life, but I just can't seem to find enough time or desire to implement better habits. I would like to have a greater understanding of the importance of good habits.

And my soul took flight and returned with an answer...

The radiating sun that rises and sets each morning dependably creates a day followed by a night and each serves a valuable purpose in the harmonic cycles of life. As does the precisely predictable tide coming in and going out and the body's obligatory cycle of sleep and awake. Like many other cycles in life, they permeate the colorful fabric of existence and resonate through the dynamic core of the soul, instilling a deep unconscious compulsion within every life upon the Earth, to emulate and create patterns for their existence.

Your meandering life is like a sparkling river predictably flowing in a wide, well-worn channel, deeply entrenched by the translucent passage of time. Your worthy desires to make beneficial changes in your life are the periodic flooding of the mighty watercourse of your aspirations. As the river of hope runs over its banks, the fleeting abundance of water opens auspicious possibilities to cut fresh, new channels and purge the accumulated sludge of the past, even as your opportunity to create beneficial new habits and traits, forsaking the deadwood of yesterday, increases with the fullness of your desire. To forever repudiate the old habits and successfully embrace the new, your yearning for meaningful change must be more compelling than the spurious comfort of remaining within the disadvantageous, unfulfilling present state you know so well.

Every aspect of your continually evolving life is built upon an interconnecting set of governing patterns and the ruling habits they spawn. Some are beneficial and others are not, but most, even those that are irritatingly adverse, are comfortable from long familiarity. Therefore, any attempt to change patterns or improve habits is frequently abandoned before it is undertaken. It is often easier to remain within the old arrangement, even one that is unfulfilling or even harmful, than to make the extra effort and suffer the pain and discomfort often associated with change.

Nor is change, no matter how beneficial, ever accomplished with merely a single, solitary effect. Even the simplest alteration of course has far-reaching repercussions, with metamorphosing ripples spreading out and rocking many of the other accustomed modes in your life.

Looking over the precipice of potential at the scintillating peaks of promise beyond the chasm of despair, with the possibility of flying or failing in attempting a leap, quivering hearts often hesitate to abandon the barren ground they stand upon in an attempt to gain the bejeweled unknown beyond. Yet to not make the attempt to reach a higher, more rewarding mountain condemns you to sit precariously upon a forlorn, slowly eroding hill of useless habits and forgotten dreams.

Consider how many actions you take each day with nary a fair thought or care that are based upon established patterns that repeat over and over again. In truth, almost every minute of your unfolding life is dictated by customary patterns for use of time that you have set or accepted. A time to rise, a time to eat, a time to work, a time to relax, a time to sleep and many more.

You are also ruled by time-worn patterns of "how"; how to speak to peers, how to speak to employers, how to act with friends, how to study and work, how to create, how to be romantic, how to treat children. The manifestation of your life is further defined by patterns of association such as to live with a cat, a dog, both, many or none, or similarly to befriend certain types of people and to shun others. Within each life pattern, resonating habits develop which are created from the prevailing atmosphere set by the master templates you have chosen for your life.

Though it is the irrevocable nature of mankind to live within a world of patterns and habits both beneficial and detrimental, it is your blessed birthright to be the master of the pre-dispositions that dictate the manner of your existence. It is within your power to choose or consent to the molded patterns you live within. Once accepted, both the good and the bad become so well worn into your heart that it is uncomfortable to change, and so ingrained in your mind that adherence to their ever-present dictates becomes automatic and without thought. You are the master to make your choices, but once ingrained into habits, you become virtually a witless slave, fettered to that which you have chosen. Good patterns are the catalyst to creating expanding success and happiness even as bad patterns are the agitator to manifesting repeated failure and unhappiness. As either one is within your power to select and capacity to achieve, why not align with those that uplift, expand and fulfill?

Nor can you blithely ignore the necessity of creating beneficial templates in your life without suffering increasingly painful penalties. Thoughtlessly immersed in apathy or disinterest, you relinquish your right to have beneficial patterns that serve you and will by default become a slave to a destructive, downward spiral of unworthy and slothful habits, which will demand an ever increasing toll upon your daily happiness. If you allow harmful patterns a toehold in your life they will birth greater more ruinous habits, which will insidiously encroach and supplant the good, forging subtle links of noxious tyranny until one day you awake to discover you are enchained.

If you find yourself ruefully encumbered by servile habits that punish you and sullen patterns that continually drop you deeper into a pit instead of raising you up to a mountain high, you have within your latent powers the ability to discard the old darkness and embrace a new dawn. The slave to bad habits and patterns can rise up in revolt. But it is not enough to merely throw off the oppressive yoke. The human essence is so dependent upon patterns and habits that a dispossessed habit will always return unless it is replaced by a new, more beneficial choice. Habits are the boats that ferry you to destinations on the phosphorescent river of life. You cannot merely step out of one without stepping into another, lest you quickly begin to sink deeper into cold, choppy waters of emptiness. And when floundering, you are inexorably drawn back to the dubious, decrepit safety of the old rather than drown for lack of a vessel. Only by carefully selecting a new boat and purposefully traveling to a known and better destination, can you be assured of a gratifying journey of expansion and fulfillment.

If you are to grow and find happiness, you cannot ignore your bad habits forever. You must some bright day become their master instead of remaining their slave, for your noble destiny shines upon a higher path, and your beckoning potential sparkles more sublime. Yesterday is a memory, tomorrow might never be. Today is where you should make your stand, where the blossoms of your possibilities can flower, where the beauty of your soul expands.

The 5th Step

WHAT OF FRIENDSHIP?

Close friends seem to be a rare commodity. Is it me? Am I too picky or undesirable, or are true friends just hard to find?

And my soul took flight and returned with an answer...

Gaze deeply into the silvery mirror of infinity. The retrospective reflection you see is your inescapable twin and enduring life's companion, your best and truest friend. Love yourself first, in forgiving humility, with sincere objectivity, firmly supported by honesty, truth and understanding that only one who has lived the labyrinth depths of your life can have. Then, with dependable alacrity, turn and give that same clarity of compassion and depth of understanding to those who would be your dearest friends. From such a firm foundation, an uplifting relationship of harmonious souls that spans the passing of time can be built.

You will sift through the inconsequential chaff of many empty acquaintances before you discover a meaningful enduring friend of enlivening depth, common interests and harmonious vitality. One who will stand with you even in the greatest storms of life. But the chaff will blow away at the first light wind of steaming adversity or blustery tempest. Some flitters about longer, but in the end, because they have no significant substance, they will swirl away into nothingness, leaving you alone. Throw them high so they are carried away quickly, that your time is not squandered in fruitless experiences or idle chatter.

A friend has a bonded resonance of enduring allegiance. Neither the foreboding gloom of the deepest darkness of night nor the raging howl of the life's most fearsome storms can move them from their deep-seated place at your side. Like mirages of supine emptiness false friends will casually abandon you amidst the tremors of your troubles, while a true friend unhesitatingly is compelled from love and loyalty, to ever lend supportive, beneficial action in your tumultuous hours of need.

Be everything for your friend that you would have them be for you. For love and time unselfishly given to a steadfast friend of merit is returned many fold. As you need gentle solace and peace, a friend is there. As you ask, a friend replies; words of encouragement, words of praise, words of caution or admonition that only from a friend would you listen and heed. How precious is such non-judgmental refuge? How valuable is such honest council? A friend is a radiating gem of immense value. In truth, because you cannot purchase the loving shelter and unfiltered wisdom of a friend, but only earn it by your worthiness and selfless reciprocation, it is priceless.

A consummate friend has no need to speak. In their trusting eyes you see the depths of their soul and they see yours. With such intuitive connections, there is often more power in soft silence, more replenishment in mutual reflection. Their mere presence revitalizes, uplifts and empowers you. Without words, in honest, reciprocated friendship, all thoughts, hopes, disappointments, and dreams are respectfully cradled in a common basket, revered in a mutual quiet joy that needs no acclaim. It is continually renewed with each shared joy or sorrow, ever weaving a vivid tapestry of mutual experiences that can never be forgotten.

To what end is friendship? In truth, enduring friendship needs no overt purpose, for by its very existence it creates a reciprocating harmony that makes each day of life more fulfilling, continually helping to expand the questing boundaries of your dreams and the storied horizons of your soul.

Ask nothing of your friend except forthright honesty and ever-ready companionship.   Be gentle with their faults and cherish their virtues. Together, share moments of laughter, times of grief, moments of challenge, pinnacles of happiness, new adventures and profound experiences unabashed and unbounded. Give your dear friend the best of all you have, especially your time. Go to them when you are full as well as when you are empty and your fullness will always be more.

The 6th Step

WHAT OF TRUE LOVE?

I have always been captivated by the romanticized version of love. Am I being corny to think it is possible to have and sustain the reality of such a love?

And my soul took flight and returned with an answer...

The delicate flower of new love is blushed in innocence. It bestows soft, sweet caresses that rapturously quicken the heart with coursing, carefree passion. The romantic love of two hearts reverberating in harmony and desire is an intricate flower, rare and beautiful, delightful and delectable. So exquisite and joyful, it beckons with a siren call that enraptures the heart and mists the mind. Were it not so, few would risk the journey in pursuit of the euphoric ecstasy and expansive, all consuming fulfillment that only an abiding love filled to its depth and breadth can bring.

The rarest form of amorous love is true love; a trustworthy, passionate embrace of enthralled lovers, joyously resonating on many levels with common foundations of life principles, embellished by shared and varied interests. Such a love is clothed in sublime majesty and destined for great treasures of fulfillment discovered in a memorable life forged together.

True love is an aspiration of many but a realization of few. It is nurtured on sacred ground in a sanctuary atop a mountain high. There is a well worn path that leads to an ancient door. Behind the imposing portal, the magnificent flower of true love blossoms in all of its glory and splendor. But only for two hearts that beat as one, whose united light of pure love can pierce the mists of confusion and contradiction that enshroud the flower of myth and legend, so that they may return with it to the world.

Many search all their lives for true love and never discover its rapture or even the path to its door. The trail is convoluted and treacherous. Many are the dangers that lurk at every bend anxiously awaiting the opportunity to pull those who would aspire to such lofty dreams to the ground and leave them barren and forlorn. Alas, how many seekers have been battered and broken for not comprehending that the journey cannot be sought or won alone. There is no force no matter how immense in power that is great enough to open the door to true love alone. Nor are there any amount of riches, fame, flattery or dutiful deeds that can pry open even the tiniest of cracks to the imposing portal. If there are two lovers and one seeks a higher, more expansive love and the other does not, the door to true love simply will not open, and the journey should not be embarked upon, for it will only end in abject frustration and utter rejection.

True love spreads forth its arms only when two hopes meld into one dream, when unconditional love is reciprocated unconditionally, when love for the beloved is as important as love of self, when the hands of two lovers clasped tenderly together with reverence and thankfulness jointly open the fabled door. When each gives all to the other, both win everything. Bridges across the daunting chasms of life are securely built when one holds the nail, the other wields the hammer and both carry the lumber.

Once the rainbow-hued flower of love is held jointly and tenderly in your grasp, know that it is not the end, only the beginning. The enrapturing bloom of love is the most sensitive and demanding of all the scented blossoms in the garden of paradise. To bless you with bounteous flowers, never ending in number, each amazingly splendid and captivating, you must cultivate, nurture and treasure it. You must never tire of its unparalleled beauty nor its intoxicating fragrance, and with thankful wonder and gleeful delight, continually find joy and fulfillment with each new radiant blossom true love reveals.

Think not that this path is easy, for where the reward is so grand, great too is the effort required to reach and retain this most precious of treasures. At times love will shake you to your core, but so too will it uplift you to heights unimagined. Love will sometimes prick you in pain and discomfort, vanquishing all facades, but so too will it comfort you when all the world falls upon you and gently soothe you with a nurturing balm of support that heals all wounds.

Love will be blind at first and see you through a gaily tinted glass. It will ignore your blemishes and will magnify your virtues. As time passes the glass will clear. Your imperfections will become obvious, your merits may recede, but true love will esteem you even more, perceiving your true essence and realizing with blissful contentment that the unvarnished reality is more adored and cherished than the imagined mirage.

Ask nothing of love but to have it willingly reciprocated. The harmonic reverberation that occurs with reciprocated love will transform you. It will uplift you. It will make you more than you ever could aspire to otherwise. You will be blessed with a singular warmth that rhythmically stirs your luminous soul as love flows in and love flows out.

Love unconditionally, without judgment for any grievance big or small, insignificant or great. For judgment and love are like oil and water, they are not compatible and you must choose one or the other. There is no place for judgment in a life of love nor can there ever be love in a life of judgment.

Love is the divine vitality of life and the everlasting light of the universe. As you love and are loved, you are a ray of pure sunshine that lightens and fills the hopeful lives of all whom you touch.

True love is extraordinary. Never take it for granted and it will never fail you. Love abundantly, with passion and tenderness and it will always be at your side. Walk hand and hand along eternity's path and true love will always light the way. Ever nurture and revere it and it shall continually enrich and uplift you beyond the celestial rainbow.

The 7th Step

WHAT OF MARRIAGE?

Marriage seems to be an endangered institution assaulted by a combination of quick divorce as soon as times get tough and many couples choosing to never get married in the first place. Some people think there are more downsides than up. What is the true value of marriage?

And my soul took flight and returned with an answer...

When you love, sweet and pure, and desire to always bask in the enlivening glow and enduring warmth that only such love bestows, you may yearn to enter into the consecrated covenant of marriage, to enshrine the light of love that supports your cherished dreams and everyday tenderly lifts the careworn spirits of life. A noble desire, but consider well before you step, for marriage is the highest level of commitment to another person, a sacred trust between blended lives and depending upon diverse factors both before and after, it will forever change you for better or worse.

If love is the refining fire that presents you with an abundant reward more valuable than pure gold, then marriage is the intricate and fabulous design created from a purposeful partnership of master jewelers, melding the unadorned gold of love into a magnificent treasure that will endure for gratifying years of continual wonder and joy. But it is a dreamy destiny, only possible in a grounded union anchored in mutual respect, navigated with common interests and ideals, uplifted by an expansive shared vision of tomorrow and empowered by a passionate desire to create it together.

Of all life's gauntlet of challenges, none shall be greater than creating an enduring, fulfilling, continually uplifting, nourishing and expanding marriage. It can become your most terrifying failure or your greatest triumph and most enduring legacy. When anxious frustrations and perplexing quandaries surround and buffet you, assailing your delicate love with unfounded fears and uncertainties, remember the wondrous qualities that brought you together and stoked the incomparable fires of love in your heart. Hold fast to that which you know is true and enduring. Pull each other through the haze of fretful turmoil. Hand-in hand part the clouds of restless doubt and know with the purity of your heart that the brilliant sun of your loves' promise is always waiting for you beyond the mist of disquietude.

The marriage of two independent and distinct lives, each with their own foundation, abilities and aspirations, is an astonishing voyage of enlightenment and personal growth, not a casual destination of convenience or a mere fanciful moment in time. Sacred vows promised are simply the first breaths on a journey of ultimate discovery. To share the rainbow sunset that warms the soul after the passage of a life fulfilled together, you must nurture love through the passing years and treasure each day you see your beloved's face.

You will have sore challenges that will try your patience, but so too will you have exalted joys that fill your heart with an upwelling love that beckons a soft smile and brings warm tears of happiness to your eyes. And when the rising sun shines bright and the warm Earth provides in generous bounty, hold hands in quiet tenderness. Softly gaze with contentment and humble thankfulness upon the adoring face of your beloved, until in the merging of your two spirits you see the opalescent lights of your lover's soul, dancing in the twinkle of their eyes.

Remember always that you are twin flames in a shared but ever-changing fire of life. As your flames dance joyously together each must still retain its own power. Each must be capable and encouraged to create its own space and not be consumed by the other, nor have its' light dimmed by the expanding shadow of its mate. May you ever stoke the fires of love, success and joy within the each others heart, and ever have your flickering fires rekindled by the radiance of each others presence when the pressing cares of the world would darken their ebullient lights.

Blessed love can become a joyful passage to the fulfilling sanctuary of marriage with an abiding commitment to a shared journey and a tender devotion to the others happiness. It is a union producing a flowering tree of destiny; soon to be brimming with the full spectrum of life lived, resolutely growing together in a steadfast harmony of purpose, with an abundant depth and breadth gained from facing all the challenging seasons of life together.

Though storms swirling about may buffet and howl, the ever blossoming tree of marriage remains, buttressed by roots that spread deep beneath the Earth, anchoring, faithful and steadfast. Its' mighty trunk holds every precious memory of life; lessons learned from times past, wisdom to build tomorrow's promise. Its spreading branches caress the invigorating morning beams of sun, lingering in warmth till the fading light of dusk and sagely measuring the journey amidst the twinkling stars of night.

May your marriage be such a magnificent flowering tree of destiny; expanding in unspoken majesty with each passing season, planted by twin souls in passionate love and sealed with hope that it may ever blossom, comfort, provide and nourish the love, commitment and dreams that gave it life.

The 8th Step

WHAT OF CHILDREN?

It is sometimes scary to contemplate bringing children into the world. Not just from assuming the 18+ year responsibility to care and nurture them, but depending upon where the parents live and their educational and financial situation, the lives of the children can be quite dangerous and deprived of many essential things. Overpopulation also has to be thought about as some places already have more people than their resources can sustain. What should be considered when contemplating bringing children into the world?

And my soul took flight and returned with an answer...

Children are the most radiant gems of heaven. Marvel in their glory and be humbled in their brilliance, for in a little child are the keys to life and happiness.

You should cherish them forever, but you can never own them or live again within their lives. They are independent spirits of tomorrow and their future is beyond the veil of your years. Teach them well, nurture them with love while they are in your care and they will bless you with treasures beyond price for all of your days.

As the vineyard master gently tends his grapes with unabashed love and endearing joy that they may produce a wine of exquisite taste, so too are you the steward of the promise of the tomorrow your children.

Verily, all those that walk the diversity of the Earth in thoughtful maturity are parents, even the barren. And all the little ones of the teeming world, even those in far-off lands, are your children. You have a responsibility to their welfare and the quality of their present, for that which you nurture creates the future you will inherit. Some will care for you and provide for you in the twilight of your life and whether others choose to have peace or strife, to work for unity or hostility, will directly and indirectly affect the color of your sunset.

Two priceless gifts are yours to bestow upon your children. More rare than the most esteemed gems of kings, yet more common than the sands of the endless desert; all parents, both the rich and poor possess them, yet all the riches of the world cannot replace them. They are precious beyond measure, for only those of selfless heart, with a vision spanning beyond their life, will ever faithfully present them to their children. The first gem is your time, which is the touchstone by which children assess the depths of your love. Each day is its own opportunity and if you lose it, like the sands of the hourglass, it can never return to you the moments lost. Its companion is your character and the example of your life, for it is the template by which your child will grow or falter. Though you may teach worthy precepts, unless your words are followed by your deeds, they will have no more value than an empty wind upon a calm sea.

Children are innocently curious and wondrously eager. Lead them with thoughtfulness into earnest discovery of the world unknown, and follow them in peace and joy into rediscovery of a carefree time you may have forgotten. As you enlighten them layer upon layer in the intricate ways of life, do so with laughter and playfulness that you may lift the weight of your own life's travails, and ever recall that the expediency of existing is not the same as the vibrancy of living.

You are the mighty catapult to their future, built with toil and sacrifice, piece by piece, year by year until at last it stands upon the mountain high. Children are the stones once dull and plain, but now polished clear and brilliant by the tumbles of life. They are breathlessly poised to take flight to the distant stars of their effulgent dreams. With joy and selflessness, cut the rope that binds them still. Leaping enthusiastically skyward they shall fly free; transformed by your loving stewardship from a sparkling stone, shaped and formed, into a magnificent, multi-colored bird of independent destiny.

Know too that all good deeds reciprocate in harmony. If to your children you are true, in their love they shall honor you. In lifting them you also gain. Each step they make you will grow the same.

The 9th Step

WHAT OF HAPPINESS?

I think every person has an ultimate goal to "just be happy", yet very few people seem to achieve a state of happiness for other than for brief moments. Are there secrets to continual happiness?

And my soul took flight and returned with an answer...

Happiness is sought by all, tantalizingly tasted by most, but a constant companion only of those who accept and are in flowing harmony with themselves. For most people, happiness is a beautiful, beguiling phantom, teasing with dizzying heights of joy and fulfillment, only to leave them dazed and melancholy when it dissolves into the turbulent mists of life.

The elixir of happiness once tasted is forever sought. Yet, the greater the pursuit the more distant it becomes for it is not a destination nor a prize to be won, but a humble love of self, a principle of mind and a way of life. It is not found at the end of the winding road but in each step of the journey along the way. It does not dwell in exotic, faraway places to be discovered on tomorrow's journey, but swells inside of your loving heart and tranquil mind, surrounded by the blessings that are already yours, waiting to be savored today. Go on a grand voyage of inner discovery and find it there, for it is futile to seek it elsewhere.

To embrace happiness as an uplifting and faithful companion, you must distinguish between passing pleasures and enduring inner joy. The fluting melody of a bird, while delightful, is here one moment and gone the next, while the satisfied happiness that emanates from within always sings.

If your life is merely a pursuit of happy moments gleaned from association with other people, or experiences beyond yourself, your fragile cup will be empty more often than full, continually leaving you thirsty for more and unsure of where to find the next drink. Like the unpredictable wind, happy moments bestowed from sources beyond your own inner glow, come and go and whither they can be found at any moment is a mystery. In the glimmer of transient happiness you are merely a vagabond searching for a warm breeze to touch your face and lift your life for an illusionary breath in time.

If worry rules your thoughts and frays your nerves there will be no home for enduring happiness within you; for each is repugnant to the other. Truly, worry is the most fruitless of endeavors. It saps the time and energy of the present to uselessly fret about a future that may never materialize. Center yourself by discovering the everyday bountiful joys of the present and the many walls of worry that exclude happiness will crumble to dust, letting in the light.

The radiance of inner happiness is not subject to events real or imagined, nor can it be given or taken away by the action of others. When you glow within, even the darkest night causes only a passing flicker and cannot dim your light.

Lasting, enduring happiness, fills your body, keeps a smile on your face and peace in your heart even on the gloomiest days. It is not a mercurial emotion but an attitude of oneness and pleasure with yourself that permeates the soul. It comes not from being a beggar to the fickleness of fate or actions of others, but from a mental state in which you love and accept yourself and acknowledge that you alone are the master of your destiny. As the master you deserve happiness and you grant it to yourself.

Yet, even the most cheerful soul has times of sadness. That

is part of the balance of life. There are shadows lurking even within the brightest joys. But they only have power to push you down if you dwell upon them. Choose to keep your face basking in the sunshine and you will only see the light. The lurkers of disquietude will languish in anonymity, unacknowledged and unmanifested.

Whenever happiness does momentarily fade away, you can bring it back quickly if you choose. Realize that your emotions are like points on a compass guiding the direction of your great ship of life. Though contrary winds may try to blow your vessel hither and yon, as the captain of your intrepid ship you have the power at any time to turn the vacillating wheel to a course of your choosing and fill your sails with a warm, favorable wind, by simply commanding it to be so and then faithfully obeying your command.

Happiness does not just happen to you. Each day you must choose serenity over agitation, enthusiasm over apathy, gratefulness over discontent, cheerfulness over melancholy, praise over criticism, laughter over wrath, confidence over cowardice, optimism over pessimism and reveling in today's joys, over waiting to find happiness in the quixotic mist of tomorrow.

Travel through life thoughtfully with a gentle smile and an easy grace that abiding contentment may have time to walk with you. Keep your veritable compass of happiness pointed true and it will always be there for you.

The 10th Step

WHAT OF PLAY
AND RELAXATION?

I know I work too hard. I put off many things I know I should do, both for myself and others, but I need to spend so much time working just to keep ahead of the bills that there's not much time left for anything else besides sleeping and eating. Am I shooting myself in the foot thinking I am helping myself and my family by working so diligently?

And my soul took flight and returned with an answer...

You are like a mighty river flowing in majesty down to the azure sea. At times the river runs fast and tumultuously, others days it gently meanders with languid leisure and grace. In the larger bends, the water frolics playfully in the shallows, tinkling and rippling with excitement as it flows over many small, rounded rocks. Whenever its long run depletes its power, the river slows to rest in deep, quiet pools and shimmering, reflective lakes, revitalizing its energy before resuming the relentless drive to its destiny.

Each aspect of the river is necessary for its health and vitality. To only flow rapidly would soon expend its essence, leaving it gasping in meager trickles. To merely meander slowly would doom it to never fulfill its great potential. If it remained always playing in the shallows, it would never have depth and majesty. If it exclusively laid still and reflecting, it would soon stagnate from inactivity.

In the river of your life do you nourish all of the aspects of your being that you may fulfill your potential and reach your destiny? Too often in the bustle of work and responsibilities, living becomes merely existing, ceasing to be a life of fulfillment and growth, dejectedly regressing to a shell at best and a cage at worst. Each day becomes a hapless martyr's path of circular futility, with one leading to the next which was the same as the prior and will be duplicated by the morrow.

The cycle of forlorn activity is broken by partaking of the fountain of play with the ones you love and the river of life is reborn in the spring of soothing relaxation and quiet reflection in the places you cherish.

The little child that you once were dwells within you still. As the child lived to play so must all play to truly live. Not competitive play that can sour rather than sweeten you, but play just for the pure joy and delightful abandonment of playing. Gleeful, unstructured frolicking, where smiles abound, spontaneous laughter is king and friends and family are bonded by shared experiences of zestful cheer and pure joy.

If play is a secret of rejuvenation and youth, then easy laughter is its twin. Merriment strengthens the heart, preserves youthful countenance and keeps the radiance of optimism sparkling brightly in your eyes. A hearty laugh is sunshine upon the soul that warms hearts, melts barriers and makes better friends of all.

Among the myriad creatures of the Earth, only humans can laugh. All other traits are shared by many of the diverse animals of the world. They too can love, find happiness, experience sadness, have and nurture families, be territorial, playful, angry and blissful, but only those born of men and woman can laugh.

Laughter is a divine gift. It is a healing balm of heart, body, mind and soul. Laugh often and with ease and your days shall be long upon the land.

If play is the fountain of youth and laughter is the sun within; quiet, carefree, relaxation is the solace of the soul. Gently resting the mind and body, releasing all cares and worries for a moment in time, is a heavenly well of energy that recharges and reinvigorates all aspects of life.

A simple, single, deep breath through the nose, with eyes closed, fingertips touching and palms pressed lightly together, followed by a prolonged exhale through the mouth, relaxes the body and calms the nerves, especially when the rush of events or crush of responsibilities dictates that there is "no time" to relax.

Melting into a hot bath, accompanied by soft lighting and melodious music, is a massage to the body's spirit.

Sink into the softness and warmth of your bed and blissfully close your eyes. Take a long, full breath and slowly exhale as you drift into a deep, restful sleep. A full, long sleep each night, where you can fly in the clouds and soar among the stars of your dreams, will be a refreshing wind of renewal for your body, mind and emotions. Yesterday's troubles can melt away, while a new spring of hope blossoms in the beams of morning sunshine.

Time away from all that is normal and everyday clears obstacles within that have held you back and returns you to your tasks with clearer judgment and renewed enthusiasm. But you need travel no further than the silence of a favored private spot, the solitude of your garden or the warmth and languid pleasure of your bath.

Resting the mind after a time of complex thoughts, allowing it to simply be empty, with no demands upon its powers, will often unlock a door to sudden intuitive insight, appearing as a brilliant light in a darkened room, unveiling answers to questions you had not asked and could not fathom.

A brief, bare connection to the natural Earth, will recharge your energy with a gentle jolt of oneness with the universe. Lay upon the soft, warm, green grass, beside the gentle murmur of a stream, looking up at billowy clouds making shapes from your daydreams. Feel the life-giving warmth of the sun radiating upon you, filling your body from head to toe. Release your cares and worries to float away upon the balmy breeze and when you arise you will have a lightness to your step and freedom in your soul.

From time to time, journey alone to venerable wells of solitude and harmony to renew your connection to the planet that sustains your life.

~ In ancient forests of towering trees, smell the pungent air, embrace the forest giants and let the peace of the ages flow gently into you.

~ On a bright summer day, call upon a waterfall of power and grandeur. Stand beneath it; feel the roar that resonates in your heart while its soft mist quietly covers you, soothing and invigorating your soul.

~ Climb atop a mountain high where the vista stretches out beyond the sky. Feel the energy of the great Earth drawing up through the peak and know that as limitless as is the view, so too are you.

~ On a clear, warm night, travel to the sand dunes of the sea. Feel the stirring in your spirit as the swirling sound of the ocean waves rushing to the shore falls upon your ears. Lay upon the innumerable sand grains of crystal and shell that were born before the time of man began. Gaze into the heavens at the endless stars that sparkle as diamonds in the dusky night and know that you are far more than a life that will come and go. You are a part of the sparkling tapestry of forever and a scintillating jewel of the hallowed Earth. Reflect upon yourself, hold revered council with the immutable stars and humbly discover who you really are.

The 11th Step

WHAT OF HEALTH?

Actively working for continued and better health is the last thing I take time for even though exercise, diet and other healthy habits are mentioned in something I read, hear or see everyday. But I do not enjoy exercise and don't have the time to prepare super healthy meals or spend 8 hours sleeping every night. How important are these things really?

And my soul took flight and returned with an answer...

Yor miraculous body is an incomparable temple of luminous, living light. If you take prudent care of your physical abode it will take marvelous care of you. But if you profane your own temple of wonder, what solace can it then give to you? Revere and cherish your tabernacle of your flesh, as is its due and it will bless you with radiant health, zestful vigor, youthful countenance and extended longevity.

You are the High Priest of the golden temple that bears your name. You alone decide what will enter it or be forbidden, how it shall be adorned and how it shall be perceived by others. Within its hallowed sanctuary it has the power to grant you physical, mental and emotional well-being in proportion to the love, care and devotion you give to it.

Give thanks, for you have been given a most magnificent body in which to house your eternal spirit during your Earthly sojourn. It has astounding recuperative and regenerative powers. If loved and nourished with good foods, sufficient nightly sleep, and respected and maintained with temperate habits and conscientious care, your body will reward you with the power to pass smoothly and vigorously through the tumultuous currents and eddies of affliction, infirmities and the challenges of life.

Maintaining your body's health and vitality by making wise choices of diet, habits, and exercise is a manifestation of gratitude for your opportunity not only to have a life, but to have the blessing of life in an awe inspiring world of beauty and splendor. And it is all the more so when you have good health and bountiful vigor to experience and enjoy its transcendent wonder and majesty.

Many will say, "I have no time to exercise, to sleep an adequate time or to prepare wholesome foods". Yet to not do these things insures that time which would have been yours to live, love, laugh, grow and have joy, will diminish, and days you would have had to walk the Earth will be taken away. The sunset of your life will come before it was due, all because of choices and decisions made by you.

For someone to claim they have no time to properly care for their body, the singular vehicle that allows them to walk, to talk, to think, to work and to enjoy a myriad of delightful pleasures, is a hollow argument at best and a self applied insult at worst. It is like a baker who feels it really doesn't matter what ingredients are used to make bread, or a mountain climber deciding it is not important to take care of the rope and climbing tools. Nor do your actions affect you alone. The shadow or light of the choices you make create consequences that also fall upon those who love and care for you. Never forget that the decisions you make each day about how to treat your body, will come back to haunt you or to bless you, and those who love and depend upon you, as surely as the night follows the day.

Neither assume nor accept that progressing age is a sentence to sharply decreasing physical or mental abilities. Your body does not stop working simply because you are getting older. Rather it creaks and groans and become a shell of its former glory because you stopped pushing and demanding that it give you more. If you substitute ease for effort today you will reap degeneration for rejuvenation tomorrow.

In pursuit of health be mindful of balance. Good health encompasses not just the physical body, but the mental and emotional as well. Life is meant to give joy and fulfillment, but too severe a regimentation of diet or exercise can become a great weight, imprisoning your pleasures and growing more tedious and tiresome than illness. And what is the value of health, if it is purchased at the price of continual anxiety and with an absence of the sweetness and savor of life?

The tempests of life can toss you helpless and powerless upon the winds of fate like a fragile autumn leaf before a winter storm. But in your health, you have a rare aspect of life in which you are truly the master of your simmering destiny. You make compelling choices every day. What is your choice today, master?

The 12th Step

WHAT OF SUCCESS?

I am a very hard worker and I have tried many entrepreneurial ventures with none showing sustained success. I'm not getting any younger. What do I have to do to rise above the dead end of day-to-day subsistence?

And my soul took flight and returned with an answer...

A luminescent fire burns within your resplendent depths; a kindling passion to be more than who you are. For many, a reality hoped for, a truth not yet seen. Oft times the troubles of life howl with chilling winds upon your guiding flame, blowing you down and dampening the effervescent light of hope. Some moments only faint embers are left glowing ethereally, clinging expectantly, waiting for your steadfast fortitude to fan the flames of true desire once more. Upon this crossroad of the future pass the great judgments of introspection and life. Many relinquish their tenuous hold to the luminous majesty they could create; their flickering fire goes out never to be rekindled and they live and die in forgotten mediocrity. But brave champions of noble mien, with sprites of fire still dancing in their gleaming eyes, determined not to live and die as they began, rise again to joust with the sardonic vicissitudes of fate.

Success in any worthy endeavor begins with the daunting heroes and dastardly villains of thoughts, hopes and fears dwelling within the recesses of your remarkable mind. Even as you are the arbiter of your health, more so are you the master of your thoughts and the provocative attitudes that proceed from them. With health, despite all that you may do, painful misfortune can still knock on your door. But not even one aimless thought enters your mind that you did not put there by choice or allow to reside there by impassive default. Your thoughts are the catalytic pathways to your actions and if you would attain grand success crowned with fulfilling personal growth and expansion, you must build uplifting trails to your cherished dreams.

Everyday miracles begin with a strong, positive state of mind that allows no quarter for pessimism and has no time for naysayers. It matters not where you stand today. By chipping away and discarding encrusted negativity within your mind and replumbing the labyrinth depths of your inner thoughts with clear goals and positive attitudes you can improve any aspect of your life and land upon gleaming stars that were previously beyond your reach.

Pessimism and its cousin criticism may be comfortable shoes from a lifetime of wear but they never carried anyone on a path to success or greatness. Pessimists never sailed off the flat Earth to discover splendid lands unknown. They never discerned secrets of the heavenly stars, built gleaming cities, or braved their life to wrest a prize from chance and fate. They never discovered who they were or what could be. They never found their sparkling destiny.

Pathways of good thoughts and positive attitudes dwindle to hollow dreams and empty yearnings unless you embark upon the remarkable trails they blaze for you. Although you may see the jewel-incrusted crown of victory in your mind, only wise choices and sure actions will bring it to your hand. When the road forks, as it always will, and a measured choice must be made of an essential deed or an unwavering course of action, listen closely to the whispering wisdom of your mind and deeply feel the embedded passions of your heart. Then choose that which resonates with both and has abiding significance.

Failure to take action, to continually plan and plot but in lame procrastination never move, is to be haunted by ghostly fears of failure that immobilizes your wavering will and terrorize your fleeing dreams. Action alone can disperse the inner doubts and shore up tremblings of the heart. The moment you act, fear quivers, for it knows that its time is numbered. With every step forward you quell the flutters of the heart and buoy the doubts of the mind, until in but a twinkling of the eye, fear and doubt have been usurped by quiet confidence and satisfying achievement.

Have the audacity to imagine great dreams and the daring to make them reality. Today is the day, and where you stand is the place to begin creating the fulfilling life you deserve.

Once propelled to action do not hesitate or desist until the sun sets on a worthy achievement. There will be ample time to enjoy the fruits of your labor once the harvest is done, but neglect your orchard while it is blossoming and the harvest shall leave you empty and wanting. The most significant differences between those who achieve grandly and those whose great dreams never materialize is not the size of their dream but the intensity of their desire, steadfastly manifested with an unwavering, energetic dedication toward attaining their chosen goals.

Certainly the formidable path to great success is the one less traveled, for it demands an exacting toll that many are unwilling to pay. Whether you are striving to rise in your chosen profession or to victoriously conquer your personal inner weaknesses, there will be daunting obstacles along the way, difficult choices to make, and effort, often very trying and wrenching force of your indomitable will, may be necessary to cross the distant finish line and be crowned the exuberant victor.

Embrace the many obstacles for they are your stepping stones to improvement and the pathway to your success. An endless gentle path without ability-stretching hurdles and formidable challenges is but an endless craven circle to nowhere. It is by the immensity of the obstacles that we have a measure for the greatness of the achievement. That is why champions are so revered. Everyone who has ever made an attempt to triumphantly reach the gold ring of victory knows that champions who have won the hero's crown looked defeat in the eye and did not blink, persevered when others faltered, believed in themselves when no one else did, dared to dream great dreams and had the inner fortitude and dauntless courage to make them reality.

In the focused pursuit of your worthy goals, both the grand and the humble; do not become blind to quietly beckoning paths of less resistance. It is easy to predetermine a route to the top of the promised mountain and become so focused upon overcoming obnoxious obstacles that arise before you that you do not see easier trails diverging up the hill. Hence, you squander much of your energy and resources powering through impeding walls that could have more easily been circumvented. When you dedicate yourself with steadfast intent and purposeful action upon achieving honorable goals, you attract mighty energies and resources to aid you in your impassioned quest. They flow to you like sweet water in a parched desert. But you must be ever watchful and cognizant of what the flow may bring to aid you on your journey, for it is ever moving and opportunities presented that can benefit you often vanish as quickly as they appear if you do not seize onto them when they are before you.

It is never too late to reach for the scintillating stars. What might be waits for you still, although it may not be behind the erstwhile door you thought. Trust yourself. Believe in your illustrious dreams and in your absolute ability to fulfill them. The tumbles and black pits of yesterday matter not. Today's radiating dawn is a new slate and each blazing sunrise is a fresh opportunity to greet the future with eyes cleared, hopes renewed, and the illuminated path of endless light and enduring success beckoning.

The 13th Step

WHAT OF KNOWLEDGE?

I love learning and have had an unrealized goal to always be enrolled in a college class every semester but finding the time is often a challenge. How important is such a continual pursuit of knowledge?

And my soul took flight and returned with an answer...

The incomparable virtue of a wide-ranging knowledge that embodies both breadth and depth is a grand power that can be gently held within a most inconspicuous soul, but come forth in mighty ways. It is a splendid rainbow of glimmering light that can dazzle and humble even the mightiest monarchs of the land.

To have the opportunity to learn of things unknown is the cocoon of education from whence the splendid butterfly of true knowledge retained and utilized may emerge, if coaxed with love and open-mindedness. But beware not to blindly accept knowledge gleaned as unquestionable truth. Simply because knowledge may comes to you by way of venerable teachers or respected sources, is no guarantee of its veracity. For who in ignorance knows if the mysterious sealed cocoon discovered will open to reveal a drab moth or a multi-hued butterfly of wonder? Education is simply an elementary introduction to knowledge. It consists of both the worthless and the priceless, the worthy and the unworthy. It only coalesces into a valuable treasure as you winnow the important from the trivial, the true from the false, and wisely choose to retain the precious because its guiding light illuminates your path of life.

Never forget that knowledge is merely power in potential. Only when it is balanced, comprehensive and applied to your life can it evolve into an abiding wisdom, becoming the great sifter of the wheat from the chaff, the scorching revealer of truth from falsehood, and your ever-present guardian to separate the valuable from the valueless.

At the gilded threshold of every worthy door through which you wish to pass and grow you must first forge a golden key based upon a basic, foundational knowledge previously gained. Knowledge leads to knowledge; therefore, seek it wherever you can find it and you will become rich in wisdom and wise in life. Drink copiously from the brimming fountains from which enlightenment flows comprehensive and grand, and may your insatiable thirst never be quenched. Look for it everywhere and you will find it wherever you look. For knowledge is not solely gleaned in esteemed schools and hallowed universities. It also freely manifests from keen observation of the intricacies of life, avid reading, boundless curiosity and studious inquiry into all things unknown.

There should be no forbidden doors in the pursuit of true knowledge, for it can only be found behind imposing portals to the unknown that are courageously opened. It lies not in the security of blissful ignorance, nor can it be found within comfortable prisons of prejudice or the blind passions of rabid political or religious dogma. Eclectic knowledge must be a noble and never ending quest to gain and retain important lessons learned from whatever source, into a magical, luminous elixir eagerly absorbed into the magnificence of your infinite mind. And from that radiant well of prismatic light to be energized to discover and create new and original solutions to every challenge before you, and to be self-compelled to follow the shimmering path of truth wherever it may lead.

Knowledge is a sumptuous freedom that can never be imprisoned. For this reason it is often feared and access to objective education and insightful information is curtailed by those who would be masters of the teeming masses. Ignorance is a caustic shackle that controls the people while unchained knowledge is the gleaming key that sets them free.

Tyrants fear knowledge more than menacing armies threatening their domain. For comprehensive knowledge among the people displaces empty minds of ignorance with minds full of understanding and comprehension. It is seditious and revolutionary for it opens the encrusted eyes of those who have been blind and stirs the righteous wrath of those who have been wronged.

Freedom and justice, right and wrong, good and evil; are hollow, meaningless shells if created and defined by governments, religion or institutions, without an unrestricted, well educated populous to give them legitimacy and veracity. And truth with a sound foundation does not fear knowledge; for under its grinding scrutiny truth is not ground down, but polished and shined until its scintillating brilliance is revealed.

Factual knowledge alone is insufficient to guarantee the ability to think freely or solve challenges not answered from rote. Nor is graduation from a grand university a surety that anything of value has been acquired, outside of a narrow field of endeavor. And such a limited field of vision is blind and useless in the complex world beyond the reflective walls of its restricted expertise.

Neither is a comprehensive knowledge base an insurer of wisdom, for the person that has been blessed to gain a depth of knowledge, but has no aptitude to think freely and originally from it, has no advantage over a person who never had the fortune to taste the wellspring of education or savory the enduring friendship of knowledge.

For the pursuit of knowledge to have redeeming value and be

a sizzling catalyst for wisdom it must have both all-encompassing breadth and boundless depth, unencumbered by mindless indoctrination and self-activated by inexhaustible curiosity. If it is not so, you will be as the prideful man who knew how to say hello in all the languages of the world, but in stammering shame knew nothing of the culture or people whom he addressed.

To reap the benefits from the knowledge you have gained you must be willing to challenge that which you are taught, to reasonably weigh its veracity, that it might prove itself. You must be able to thoughtfully consider a stimulating or provoking statement or situation without quickly accepting or rejecting it, and simultaneously and fairly be able to objectively consider two opposing ideas.

For knowledge to be greatly advantageous requires your ability to think beyond the limits of your education, upbringing or indoctrination, to tap into the resplendent gem of your mind, discovering within its many faceted faces flashes of the light of truth crystallized from the views and teachings of diverse sources. The ignorant alone look into the jewel of life hoping to see only their reflection.

To give validity to the pursuit of knowledge you must be free to search for it in the depths of every gentle valley and atop the heights of every craggy mountain. You owe it to yourself and your fellow travelers upon the Earth to pursue the fruits of that freedom with a life time of love and gusto. To do less condemns you to live a flickering shadow of your towering potential and deprives the world, which must continue with less than the promise of your resplendent light.

The 14th Step

WHAT OF PASSION AND SERENITY?

I can get very enthused about things and some people feel I get over exuberant. When I am very excited about something I get so focused I sometimes happily neglect responsibilities in other areas. Is there an optimal emotional state to strive for?

And my soul took flight and returned with an answer...

Amid hushed anticipation the imminent landfall of a formidable hurricane reverberates with a primordial resonance within the anxious hearts and minds of those in its path, even as it fills them with unforgettable awe and spine-tingling wonder. Unlike lesser winds that have no substance or stamina and are easily rebuked, no mustered force of man or nature can deter the mighty cyclones from their chosen path of destiny. For the unconquerable titans of the restless sea are centered from within by a placid calm, allowing them to increase and sustain their invincible power as they whirl in primal majesty around the gentle peace and tranquil serenity of their core. Thus is the potential of the incandescent passion smoldering within you, when it is centered by a quiet serenity that resides there too.

Passion alone soon burns itself up, singeing friends in its blindness and ultimately making a fool of the passionate.

Serenity reflecting only itself quickly dulls the spirit and removes the spice from life. But focused passion, tempered by reposing inner serenity, lights glowing fires in quickening souls, making impossible aspirations achievable and dreams of effervescent fancy into elemental reality.

Passion is an effulgent gift of rainbow light touched at birth by children in blushed innocence that they may joyously feel the glee of discovery and the excitement of adventure. Serenity is imbued at birth as an opposing twin to balance the fervor of passion that both may grow in fullness. As passion is the fire that expands beyond, serenity is the still water that abides within. Serenity quiets troubled hearts, and discovers the profound in all it sees. Passion enraptures the spirit with dynamic vivacity and plants the seed of sweet euphoria. For a child, the world remains a passionate, enchanting universe only as long as their racing heart and nimble mind have a velvet cushion of inner serenity to buffer the sharp edges and painful points of their ever questing life.

Restless passion without inner serenity is like a blazing fire without the virtue of illuminating light. It burns instead of heals. Others shrink away in fear from its wrath rather than gather in inspiration to its promise. But passion cradled in serenity, accords tingling light and resonating warmth to all. Its sparkling luminance is a torch of hope and idealism that not only empowers the torch bearer but inspires and motivates all drawn to its beacon of exhilarating expectancy.

Though serenity is the grounding center, passion is the expanding power. Before the first notes of celebrated musical masterpieces were written, passion enflamed the heart of the composer. Before the first magnificent inventions of the modern era were conceived, passion stoked the resourcefulness and innovation of the mind of the inventor. A life enlivened by passion puts sparkles in the eyes and opens sealed doors to paths unimagined. As passion courses through your veins new opportunities unfold before you.

Passion releases the latent wizard within and magic crackles in the air as the irrepressible force of your exuberant desires forms and coalesces into a magnificent manifestation of your erupting ideas. Passion is nothing less than the compelling catalyst from which apathetic mediocrity becomes spellbinding greatness.

Alas, the flame of passion, unchecked by the calm and peace of serenity, frequently transforms into a fire of escalating irrationality often followed by an exploding inferno of reasonless, indefensible anger. In disagreements between people, scorching anger is often used when truth, facts and logic cannot support the argument or when one lacks the intellect to articulate a well-founded position. Shouting another person into submission, concession or tears only plants the seed for a sorrowful retribution and makes a shameful mockery of the valorous virtues and true nobility of passion.

Though one may search far and wide for soothing waters of serenity to quench the fires of self-destructive anger, a well of calm and peace will never be discovered except within the depths of one's own heart, mind and soul, where it ever awaits to embrace with love. If it cannot be discovered there, it is fruitless to search elsewhere. Like stagnant water in a putrid pool, the source of the venom is within. Only in accepting that truth will the door to inner harmony swing open with an invitation of solace, to savor the refreshing mists of serenity and drink from the pure, flowing, crystal fountain of the soul once more.

Many people seek money and success with reckless intensity when they would be better served to be pursuing all aspects of life within a scintillating aura of serenity. Of what use is a house of gold built at the price of neglected friends, damaged health, forsaken love, forgotten children and irretrievably lost joy and happiness? How many cherished memories could have been, that never were?

Success and serenity can be harmonious if they flow forward on the path of life lovingly intertwined. Success does not have to be gained at the sacrifice of all the sweetness and divinity of life. The fuel of success is passion, and serenity is the unimposing container that can cool its explosive power in a calming embrace of quiet and solitude. By this compelling kinship, the force of burning passion may be ignited in continued rhythmic intensity and not consumed in a brief bursting pyre of glory or infamy.

Inner serenity is highlighted with a cheerfulness of spirit reflected in an easy smile, eyes of glimmering humor and an ever gentle countenance as warm and delightful as sunshine amidst the colorful flowers of summer. To attain inner serenity you must find a place of tranquility and silence within yourself and accept and affirm that you are a beautiful, wonderful being of light who does not need to be uplifted by other people or events, nor need the world to give you hope, for the brilliance of the rainbow is contained within you. Nor is there a need to travel to any place beyond the chair you sit in, the bed you lay upon, your sweet smelling garden or your warm, luxurious bath. Enduring inner serenity is not bestowed by a guru or discovered in a distant land, but steadfastly waits for you where you now are, within the sanctity of your own heart, mind, body and soul.

A noble quest to commune with the celestial core of serenity whispering within your soul is an essential journey of self discovery. Searching and connecting to the omnipresent well of lucent harmony flowing through your essence transforms you from that moment on into a more balanced individual with greater light and rising possibilities. Though frenzied activity and discombobulating chaos may still intrude upon your life from other people, events and activities, you will forever be able to closely hold a cherished inner place of quite and tranquility. It will resonate from your spirit within, reverberating through every fiber of your being, calming your nerves, clearing your mind and allowing you to think, create and act amidst disharmony, even while others falter.

Softly illuminating a life as the aurora lights the sky in rainbow hues, vivid passion and whispering serenity have preceded everything of great accomplishment in the world. Blended they become the magical cornucopia of genius. Passion communing with serenity is a mystical force of the soul that gives wings to hope and substance to dreams.

The 15th Step

WHAT OF IMAGINATION AND VISION?

I've always been accused of being a dreamer. Some people feel that is a bad thing and I should get my feet more on the ground. Is there a value in everyday life to dreams, even really big ones?

And my soul took flight and returned with an answer...

On a sparkling, clear dawn of a timeless new day, a shimmering, brilliant yellow sun of summer rises above a barren, parched desert floor silhouetting the towering, improbable enormity of the ancient pyramid of Giza as the final, smooth white capstone is placed 481 feet above the festooned crowds, surging like awestruck ants far below. Millennia into the distant future one of two brothers standing atop a nondescript sand hill, mounts an ungainly mechanized contraption created in their small bicycle shop and leaping into the ocean breeze lifts free from the bonds of Earth, soaring untethered on currents of air, into a realm reserved for birds alone since the dawn of time. Before two more generations pass, even the distant, luminescent Moon of romance, eternal guardian of the ethereal night sky, separated from the planet-bound by the vast, frigid void of space, shall bear the footprints of daunting explorers. These and many other world impacting feats all began as a murmuring wisp of an idea twirling within the boundless imagination of those who dared to see that which had never been.

Alone in his sparse studio, a young man ponders a colossal block of snow white marble towering skyward four times his height just delivered from the famed quarries of the verdant mountains of Carrara. His imagination envisions the sublime form frozen inside the cold, crystallized stone waiting to be released. Then with measured deliberation, he begins to chisel, ever so carefully, freeing the incomparable perfection of Michelangelo's immortal David that swirled alive in his mind.

In a neighboring town, a wry man with a flowing grey beard sits contemplating a blank, finely sanded, board of poplar wood. Commissioned to render an elegant portrait of the wife of a local nobleman, he thoughtfully takes a brush to hand and with strikingly innovative techniques fashions a transcendent masterpiece of a beautiful, alluring young woman, adoringly known to the world as Leonardo da Vinci's Mona Lisa. His masterful rendition of her deep, brown eyes, reflecting an air of subtle aloofness and her soft, enigmatic smile, have continued to bewitch awestruck admirers for five hundred years. As with countless great artists throughout time, these renaissance masters did not see an ignoble block of stone or a simple canvas of wood. They dared to imagine the stirring magnificence of what could be and then had the enduring zeal and vision to make it reality.

Imagination is a mystical vortex of emerging dreams and latent possibilities. It can transport and transform you. It can reveal that which cannot be seen, give substance to that which was nothing, endow voice to that which was silent, fill with emotion that which was numb, raise hope in the hopeless, courage in the fearful and make kings of paupers. But its elemental magic, as powerful as any in the infinite universe, is that ideas imagined as mere mists without substance, can materialize into the quintessence of new realities.

Imagination is the relentless progenitor of a greater vision, birthing new and often radical ideas, instigating passionate actions, building an ever expanding wave of ebullient momentum, which can, in fortuitous moments of destiny, irreversibly change the slumbering world. For this reason, the seeds of unfettered imagination are often ruthlessly quashed before they are sown, by aggrandized tyrants callously ruling others by compulsion and coercion, but secretly trembling in the darkness knowing they would be exiled in infamy if truth was revealed. For even the humblest soul, once enlightened and empowered by a greater vision, is stirred by an insatiable passion for transformation that overcomes a quavering heart and mind to the point that they can never return to the world as it was. Nor can the most powerful army in the world thwart or contain a righteous truth imagined, envisioned, and sown to reap the whirlwind of destiny.

Imagination is only limited by your daring, even as the surging reality of your life is only constrained by your courage to follow through with your illustrious dreams. Do not falter if others ridicule your cherished vision. Many of the greatest ideas to grace the Earth were sodden fodder for mockery and disdain when first revealed. Know of a surety that pubescent seeds sown expectantly in your fertile imagination can bear delicious fruit if you conscientiously nurture the blossoming garden of your dreams.

Remember, when contemplating any challenge before you, from the creation of a memorable work of art to solving a problem vexing the world, the answer lays not within the familiarity of the nest that's known, but flies on wings of inspiration within the vastness of your audacious imagination, soaring on currents of ideas and solutions beckoning beyond the distant horizon.

Do not hesitate to let your infinite imagination run free for fear that there will not be much to see. Before every great person there was a great dream and before every storied marvel of art or magnificent edifice of grandeur there was a stirring ethereal vision of the wonder and beauty that was to be. Greatness always begins with simplicity, even as an unstoppable flood begins with a single drop of rain. So too, the towering patriarchs of the ancient forest, who commune each night with the twinkling stars, began as a tiny seeds quietly buried in soft obscurity beneath the nurturing sod of Mother Earth. Even as your cascading avalanche of breath-taking vision and surpassing power begins with a single snowflake of a new idea.

Life without creative imagination and expanding vision to excite and motivate is boringly mundane at best and darkly depressing at worst. But like a fog retreating before the sun, despondency evaporates before the brilliance of a new vision. Search for that which stimulates you and cultivate those ideas and pursuits which electrify your passion. The impetus of energized interest will open the opulence of your imagination and the plethora of your dreams, freeing latent capabilities, propelling you to hallowed visions of wonders unborn, and setting the stage for the birth of the divine progeny of your remarkable, incomparable imagination.

The 16th Step

WHAT OF CREATIVITY AND ART?

Though some people are natural artists I've never had as much talent as desire. But it seems like almost everyone has some means of creative expression. How important is it and why?

And my soul took flight and returned with an answer...

Tingling and swirling with welling illumination, billowing and coalescing with emerging virtuosity, a divine spark of creativity reverberates as a rhythmic stimulus of genius within every mind and an awakening quiver of passion in every heart; prodding and motivating, restlessly clamoring to be set free.

To create: oh what a beautiful fulfillment! From the immemorial dawn of time humans have marked their ascendancy by ingenious creations that give ease and comfort to their life and an astounding array of art, writing, dance, music and performance that titillate their moods and quicken their spirits.

Artistic release is the outward manifestation of the inner personality and profound soul of man. It shakes off the settled dust of mundane life and propels both the artist and the viewer to soaring new realms and introspective inner worlds. Without the uplifting, restyling, exhilarating challenge of artistic rendition, there would be no flavor and little savor to life. Art speaks in a universal language. It reaches into ones innermost depths and beguilingly resonates with shimmering currents of outer passions and secret longings. Like a sweet caress, it engenders an enduring, adoring love of the beauty and insights so subtly revealed.

In the creation of any great art, a point is reached where the inspired artist is not only deeply connected to the throbbing inner fervor and restless flux racing through their heart and mind, but also communing with a higher source of illumination and united in some mysterious way to the inner longings of the vast multitude of people upon the Earth. Within this realm of kindred oneness, profound inspiration is birthed from which transcendent art springs forth resonating with the timeless soul and enduring in vivid awe and wonder through the ages.

The ability to create exquisite art is not reserved for a gifted few, but is a wellspring of energy dwelling within every humble soul, breathlessly longing to be called upon. Everyone has a need to create, for art calls upon the deepest emotions and upwelling currents swirling within the artist's spirit, transporting them from mundane dreariness to startling perception and animation. It gives them an uncompromised venue to freely reveal that which they are unable to communicate in other ways.

To take an inner inspiration without substance and manifest it into some wondrous form of art, requires a willingness to look anew at the things that surround you in everyday life; to notice the shadows as well as the lights, to see beauty in the simplest of things. To create is to accept that you will make mistakes and to understand that errors can open wondrous doors to places you would not otherwise have visited, perhaps becoming the catalytic spark to a masterpiece.

Noteworthy creativity flourishes when the artist values originality more than conforming to prevailing styles and communes in joy with a remarkable balance of four vital energies swirling resplendently within their heart and mind; the uninhibited rambunctiousness of the inner child playing with the order and discipline of the outer adult, and the nurturing inspiration of the female dancing with the cavalier risk taking innovation of the male.

A true measure of an art piece's value is the level of its enduring fascination through the passing decades and centuries. If it still has wonder to impart after ages of time, it is a monumental testament to its stirring originality, perfection and nuanced subtleties. It communes with the soul and resonates deeply and uniquely with each person that becomes fascinatingly enraptured within its sublime majesty. There are many pieces of art but precious few timeless masterpieces. Those worthy of that title continue to inspire, enthrall and humble viewers from generation to generation long after less outstanding pieces have been stored in dark closets and forgotten.

Artistic creation is a majestic waterfall ever flowing in an endless cascade of possibilities. Each coalescing drop of water leaping in glistening spray over the breath-taking precipice is a creative embryo waiting to bring visions unborn to vibrant life. Standing beneath the showering waterfall of creativity is one of the greatest joys in the journey of life. And in the river of artistic plenitude, there is always more.

The 17th Step

WHAT OF ADVERSITY?

Everyone has adversity and I have seen it literally destroy people's lives. Is there a way to minimize the damage, or even better, minimize the adversity?

And my soul took flight and returned with an answer...

Sailing upon the boundless ocean of effervescent life, if you wish to travel from your current location to a destination of greater reward, contention with the billowing winds of adversity is an essential catalyst not merely an inconvenience to be petulantly tolerated. Even as a wise mariner cannily catches the swelling force of the quickening wind to fill the languid sails and suddenly propel his ship, so too can you use the swirling adversities of life as welcome conveyances to prodigious growth and achievement. A becalmed sea may be serenely peaceful and for a time restfully recharging to the body and soul, but when idleness is prolonged too long the listless aimlessness becomes an abyss of apathy, sucking away all the enthusiasm and joy of living.

A life without stout challenges to bring forth the finer, nobler qualities restlessly swirling within the heart and mind, will be plagued by endless unfeigned boredom and periodically jarred by a disquieted awareness of unfilled potential. Like thunder rumbling on a distant mountain, you will often sense the latent power lurking in the distance, beyond the horizon of your current reality. But to be illuminated by the light of the storm, you must first be willing to contend with the wind and the rain.

Court not adversity, but neither shirk it when it comes your way. Avoidance may momentarily seem the easier path, but blindly running from your problems does not make them blithely vanish away. Instead, your exposed weaknesses encourage your baleful adversities to return twice as strong another fateful day. Though rising challenges may stretch your latent abilities and test the mettle of your character, once conquered they are revealed as disguised stepping stones of ascension leading to your cherished dreams.

Continual resistance does not impede your desired progress, it makes it possible. Consider the colorful kites that tug relentlessly upon their strings, whipping from side to side against the blustery wind, pulling, it would seem, to be free. But cut the string, the incessant resistance ends and within moments the kite will flutter helplessly to the unforgiving Earth. Nor without continued opposition from the surging wind, will even the most lovingly crafted kite ever lift off the ground. Though you may spend many tedious hours carefully creating a most beautiful and aeronautically perfect wing of the sky, without a reliable wind to rise against, it will never fly.

Do not shirk stout challenges, as ornery or unpleasant as they may be, for you will never discover who you truly are or who you can become, until you have been immersed in the singeing fires of adversity. It is only within the purifying furnace of stinging trials and tumultuous tribulations that the true character, strength and abilities of people are revealed, even to themselves. Formidable adversity elicits latent capabilities and often startling genius that in unchallenging circumstances lays unrecognized and unborn.

Neither should you seek to have lesser challenges, but greater strength and continually evolving abilities. The more difficult and arduous the climb, the more savored and expansive will be the glorious view upon the top. And the higher the lofty mountain, the greater you become in the ascent, for it is not only the craggy peak that is conquered but also your own quavering limitations.

The enduring value of that which is acquired by persistent effort is ascertained not only by its intrinsic worth but also by the level of difficulty in acquiring it. Easy acquisitions and patronizing accolades bestowed after only slight travail are appreciated little, while those obtained only after strenuous effort and serious intent, retain lasting worth and cherished meaning. In gaining them you expand the circumscribed boundaries of your self esteem and enlarge the whispered promise of your possibilities.

Multifaceted adversity is the never ending grind stone of daily existence. It can wear you down until all that remains is the hapless powder of a promising life that once was, blowing away forgotten in a nameless wind, or it can sharpen and polish you, honing your innate abilities and creating a magnificent testament of diverse accomplishments that bear your noble name. You are the ultimate master, decreeing by your measured decisions and chosen actions each day whether testy challenges and trying adversities will abrade you into dust, or shine you up into brilliance. What is your steadfast resolution?

Certainly there are some challenges so daunting that wisdom gives pause, some calamities so wrenching that the trembling soul is torn in anguish. In stinging moments like these, reflect deeply upon your purest essence. Remember who you are and that your singular life has a meaningful purpose. There are deserving causes begging for your reassuring enthusiasm and illuminating knowledge. There are those who are calmed and uplifted by your presence, cherished in your heart, beloved and true and still in need of your unconditional love, steadfast attention, unfailing support and hearty encouragement. And many are the worthy goals both simple and grand that you have yet to achieve in your nascent life. Exuberant wonder and joy waits for you still within fragrant blossoms of possibilities that have yet to bloom. Though painful adversity may sometimes knock you down with surprising ferocity, you are only defeated if you do not courageously stand again and undaunted face the challenge anew. To do anything less is to let contemptuous circumstances and pernicious people infuriate and embitter you. Remember, you may get singed when the fiery darts of adversity zing toward you, but you will only wither and get burned if you stand idle while they strike your noble heart.

See adversity as a discordant tune to rouse your apathetic spirit, not deflate it. Rise with gusto to the cackling challenge. If weighty burdens sometimes simply overwhelm you, remember the gorgeous flowers that wilt in the cold blasts of winter winds, only to rise again in unrivaled splendor from the forgotten darkness, when tenderly caressed by the warmth of the bright spring sun that will surely come. So too, if your life is clenched in an icy, wintry grip, hold fast! Your spring is coming upon the red-hued break of day.

Endure adversity and you shall outlast it. Find a peaceful space in your heart to rejoice amidst the challenges. For within every poignant heartbreak and every stinging loss, resides a valuable and worthy lesson, containing the virgin seeds for tomorrow's bounteous joy. The gripping embrace of ill fortune, though painful in the moment, reveals the core of your transcendent character, which empowered and nourished will blossom into a rainbow-hued garden of sweet fulfillment.

When provocative obstacles and galling challenges weigh most heavily upon you, look deeper and further at the current status and circumstances of your wavering life. Often you will discover that the formidable adversities that you have endured have scraped away encrusted veneers revealing startling new opportunities.

In times of greatest tumult open your tired eyes wide for wonderful fortuity is misting around you. It is when the stygian night sky is darkest that it is most bejeweled in the scintillating stars of possibility.

The 18th Step

WHAT OF RESPECT?

I grew up saying, "yes sir" and "yes ma'am" to my elders, and addressing them as "Mr." and "Mrs." Today, in the United States it seems everyone is on a first name basis. Though I hear people speak with courtesy I seldom hear respect in their address or speech. Is it just a quaint relic of a bygone era?

And my soul took flight and returned with an answer...

To cultivate a conscientious habit of unfeigned respect for every precious life upon the bounteous Earth is one of the wisest choices you will ever make in the eloquence of your sojourn. It is a priceless gift you can freely give in generous abundance that will shower you in reciprocating bounty both seen and unseen, a thousand times over.

The luminous halo of reciprocating respect should extend to all of life, for all that lives makes everything that you have possible. Life in all its countless forms should be ever cherished and never injured gratuitously. Honor the lush green plants, tall noble trees and abundant flowers bursting with color. They give you life-filling oxygen to breathe, bounteous food to eat, shelter for your family, medicines to heal, clothes to wear and unsurpassed beauty to behold. Respect the innocent animals, birds and creatures of the sea, dwelling upon the Earth in majestic diversity. Many can become cherished friends and companions, others clothe you, some give their lives that you may continue yours and all teach joy in the simple pleasure of living.

Give loving deference to the hallowed Earth for it is the miraculous cradle of vitality, the gentle, nurturing womb from which a dazzling multitude of life springs forth. In the miracle of the verdant planet that is home to everyone, the refreshing rains fall and the temperate sun shines upon all. Equally marvelous, yet invisible and far from thought, the myriad diversity of teeming life is faithfully guarded by an omnipresent magnetic field, a multilayered protective atmosphere, a reflective ozone shield and a continually spinning revolution, which ensures every place where life dwells has a bright day to warm and an enveloping night to cool.

For respect to be given as an honorable projection of courteous quiet strength and not scorned as a twittering weakness of the fearful, you must begin with an honest esteem for yourself, earned by living a life of which you are not ashamed and manifested by the conscientious love, thoughtful care and dutiful attention you give your singular body and promising life. For you can only give a sentiment to others that you already possess. If you do not respect yourself, the respect you think you give to others will be an empty illusion without substance.

Only once you fully honor yourself with wise choices and virtuous deeds, does self-respect become powerfully imbued in your spirit. Once so placed, nobody can ever take it from you. A humble self-esteem breeds a quiet self-confidence that strengthens into the hewed cornerstone of your crystallizing potential and the firm foundation of your expanding virtue. Possession or lack of it infuses every decision you make and influences all the vicissitudes of your journey. Live your life honorably and worthy of your own unpretentious respect that you may magnanimously give it to others and gratefully see it returned in earnest appreciation.

Nor should you extend less respect, courtesy or interest to a child than you give to yourself or another adult, for they will reciprocate in heart-melting gratitude and exuberance. In their trusting innocence and with their loving desire to please, they are certainly deserving of benevolently kind and attentive respect. In their naïve adoration they will faithfully emulate the examples of your virtues or your vices. And you play God in choosing which it will be, so choose well.

So too, respect the elderly. For where they now are, in their frailties and challenges, you shall someday be. And where you now are, with the opportunities of life exuberantly awaiting, only became possible because of the selfless sacrifices of your elders who blazed the path before you. When you and the countless young men and women of the world were clamorous dependents, unable to care for yourselves, it was those who are now old that sacrificed their time and resources, showering you with warm love and dutiful attentiveness that you might stand upon the resplendent threshold of opportunity today. They and their valiant generation were bruised and broken in poignant battles of life and war, to faithfully deliver a legacy of hope and promise into your hands.

Yet respect, like the equivocal portents of the fickle weather, can be misinterpreted. It should be withheld from automatic deference simply because of noble position or high authority. For respect must be earned by virtuous and valorous actions, not given as a crown without merit. Though an individual's lofty station in life may be noteworthy, they only deserve unfeigned respect if they return it in honest sincerity to you, by their considerate words and meritorious deeds. To grant deferential respect to anyone who does not reciprocate the esteemed sentiment and conscientious action, is to cause self-inflicted wounds more grievous than the caustic pains inflicted by the callous and disrespectful.

The respect you give to other people emanates undisguised from your persona, and manifests in the sincerity, simplicity and elegance of your everyday actions. Be ever thoughtful of the words you speak and the tone in which they leave your lips.

Cultivation of genuine civility, commendable manners and conscientious behavior, coupled with mindfully using a polite manner of speech that resounds with sincerity, not artifice, will open imposing doors of opportunity and reap a harvest of appreciative goodwill.

Be generous and frequent in complementing others for their meritorious actions both big and small. When you show sincere admiration and bona fide respect for anything of excellence in another person you share in their crowning glory and radiating joy. In voicing deserving compliments rather than holding them silently inside, and showing interested appreciation of others abilities and accomplishments, deep chords are struck which resonate within the soul calling forth the best within people, motivating them to greater respect and accommodation of your own laudable desires. Your honest words of kindness have no cost but are of inestimable value. Not only do they brighten another's day, but thoughtful words of consideration and compliment can benefit both of your lives and have shimmering echoes that reverberate long after the moment has passed.

Listening fully to each word as someone speaks and attentively remaining alert to their body gestures and facial expressions with your eyes, is an essential aspect of conscientious respect. Neither your mind nor your actions can be involved in anything else if you are to give engaged attentiveness to the words and body language of another. Nor can you be listening more in your mind to what you will say next, rather than to the words the other person is speaking at the moment. Remember to always listen more than you speak and you shall ever glean greater knowledge and earn higher respect from others. Fortuitously, you were born with two sensitive ears to hear and two alert eyes to see, but only one simple tongue to speak. Therefore, silently be four times more attentive with your eyes and ears than you speak and you shall more easily ascend the vaunted mountains of wisdom, admiration and respect.

True respect also implies an unconditional willingness to

accept other people, regardless of their culture, race, politics, religion, station in life, or other notable differences. It grants them the right to freely hold and practice their culture, personal beliefs and divergent points of view, even if they do not agree with yours, provided they are not injurious to others and that the respect you give is reciprocated. This cannot be mere tolerance, for that is just prejudice wrapped in civility. True respect implies granting others the right to live as they wish, without exploitation or harassment, and in ways that may not serve your purposes or desires, as long as they are reciprocating in kind. Even if they are traveling a path you would not choose and may even find abhorrent, unless you have lived the intricacies of their life and experienced the magnitude of their challenges, you cannot know that which motivates them or understand that which fulfills them. To refuse to give others legitimate respect that acknowledges their unique persona, culture and chosen path as honorable and credible, is to manifest poignant evidence that your own position may be of tenuous merit. But to ungrudgingly grant respect and dignity to those who differ from you, is to bridge the yawing gap that divides and to travel a higher road to a more promising tomorrow for all.

In non-judgmental respect, peacefully acknowledge that the divergent path others choose may be as right for them as the momentous one you have chosen is correct for you. To achieve abiding harmony and increasing growth in your life, continually look through the translucent eyes of others and see the challenging world as they see it that you may understand their ever-present hopes, dreams, fears and motivations. Though you may still disagree, in understanding their heart-felt perspective, you will not fear that which is different and in your valor, with eyes open and heart unchained, you will light the effervescent lives of all whom you touch.

The 19th Step

WHAT OF FREEDOM AND RESPONSIBILITY?

It is easy to take freedom for granted and not even truly realize what it embodies when it is all someone has known since birth. Having traveled the world somewhat, I have been exposed to countries and communities where there is a great deal of freedom and others where there is a little less because people have voluntarily chosen to trade some of their freedom for heightened security. At the extreme, I have faced crushing barriers in dictatorships where freedom is sharply curtailed. What is the true nature and value of freedom?

And my soul took flight and returned with an answer...

Freedom, the indomitable torch of aspiring hope, radiates into the shrouded darkness and ignominious oppressions of life. Illuminated by the brilliant light of freedom, the magnificence of humanity rises to embrace the blazing sunrise of boundless potential, and the walls of pernicious suppression crash down in a thunderous tumult upon the rusted dust of yesterday's shattered chains.

Throughout history, freedom has been a catalyst for an explosion and expansion of the marvelous and progressive, conceived by adroit individuals contemplating, creating and laboring in its warm, gentle winds. The boundless inspiration of original innovation proliferates in a pervasiveness of freedom even as it is stifled in the perversion of restriction.

n all of nature including the race of man, the potential for expansive growth is limited only by the freedom available to enlarge, circumscribed by the surrounding boundaries. Consider a tree that by genetic design should grow to the size of a house, but with its roots constrained within a very small container, it will have its growth limited by inadequate space to create an expansive foundation to nurture and nourish it. So too, a person confined by a lack of a wide-ranging, quality education or other deleterious impediments, does not have the opportunity to expand to the fullness of their possibilities, beyond the maleficent walls of their damming limitations.

In the extreme, no matter how great the coursing passion, desire or talent, a person interred behind the locked walls of a prison will never write a memorable symphony, nor pen an epic story, create a world changing invention, paint an enduring masterpiece or leave any manner of shining legacy for the ages. The noblest and grandest achievements are only birthed when flying unfettered beyond the clouds of creative and intellectual constraint, soaring in the limitless sky of freedom.

Prisons of life can be just as suffocating as those of transgression. The shackles imposed by subsistence poverty, uneducated ignorance, abusive relationships, dogmatic religions and intrusive governmental oppression are prisons as numbing and restricting as those encircled by bare walls of cold stone. To unleash the magnificent potential of destiny, one must be free.

More insidious than institutional subjugation is the despairing slavery imposed by self. Undeterred desire and stirring motivation to rise above mediocrity must throb and reverberate in the heart and mind before freedom has meaning or can bear fruit. The heaviest chains are the ones people wrap around themselves. A person impoverished by a grinding lethargy of negative thoughts and limited by the apathy of uninspired attitudes, is imprisoned from their latent potential as surely as someone locked behind the steel bars of incarceration. But there is a distinct difference. With an unbridled determination to transform themselves and their unfulfilled reality, the prisoner of self holds the dynamic key to their own blissful freedom and exhilarating expansion.

The liberty to live as one desires is a natural foundation of freedom that stands upon an immutable pillar of equality without which it is merely an empty word, hollow and meaningless. Truly, freedom for one must be freedom for all. To be worthy to receive freedom you must be willing to grant it in the same measure to others, even those with whom you disagree and provide in all instances that the liberty exercised by anyone is injurious to none.

Across the world, in lands great and small, the clarion call of freedom resounds in the heart and enthralls the mind, for it is the natural state of mankind longing to boldly spring forth. Yet precious liberty won, often at the price of painful revolution and streets of blood, is soon diminished without determined vigilance and vanishes like the whispered memories of a dream from the timid embrace of an apathetic populace. It is too often the sad history and nature of entrenched governments and their leaders that when given a stewardship and entrusted with authority by the people, they ever seek to enlarge their powers and restrict and control the rights of the trusting citizens whom they are intended to serve.

The price of everlasting freedom is willing acceptance of both personal and civic responsibility. Whether gleaming in an individual life or coursing through the fortunes of a country, liberty without responsibility leads to anarchy, a powerless state of insecurity that will soon be supplanted by despotism and tyranny.

Responsibility begins with your personal life and actions. The unfettered freedom to expand and grow, to rise from mediocrity and obtain excellence, is meaningless unless you are motivated enough to reach for the possibilities and willing to shoulder the subsequent obligations. Only an unctuous cad would accept a precious gift with an ingratiating smile and then turn their back to the gift giver; and you cannot in good conscious call for freedom and then avoid the accompanying responsibilities. Freedom thus gained is not long held.

Nor should you acquiesce to the restrictions of overshadowing and overbearing security negating the opportunity to live in unshackled freedom. To do so, is to be forever haunted by the shinning life that could have been. Liberty is a priceless gem that will turn to worthless dust unless valiantly defended. To have such a gift and not take advantage of the expansive opportunities it presents, gratefully shouldering the accompanying responsibilities is to forever live in cantankerous chains forged by your own hand.

With freedom's enlightenment dawns the sometimes frightening understanding that you are solely responsible for your own life, happiness and success. The decisions you make and the actions you take directly cause the joyful benefits, or distasteful and painful consequences that ensue. There is no one else to praise or blame. Happily accept responsibility for your serendipitous ship of life. You are the rightful captain for only you can correctly navigate your course by the twinkling stars that guide your unique destiny. Accepting accountability for your life is immensely empowering and emancipating. It reveals bejeweled vistas of possibility and instills within your hopeful heart an ardent enthusiasm to fulfill the yearnings of your restless dreams.

The responsible exercise of personal liberty includes not merely avoiding harm to others, but having a heightened awareness of those things which are important, significant and beneficial both to you and your fellow travelers upon the Earth, coupled with a firm commitment to take virtuous actions even when unobserved and even when the choice is difficult. Though such valiant distinctions may not always produce accolades, their value to your self-esteem and personal growth is immeasurable.

Freedom is an intoxicating ideal and once the music resounds in your soul it is a sweet symphony ever savored and desired. Akin to the winsome song of colorful birds, joyously heralding the hopes and possibilities of the newborn spring, it beckons you with a jubilant resonance vibrating within your essence. With alert anticipation, rise up to the sounds of freedom's hope. As the rhapsody builds in sublime majesty, into a crescendo of harmonic wonder, lift your head joyously to the heavens and open your arms wide. Feel the music of freedom pulsating within your soul. With a great shout of triumph, embrace and be transformed by the brilliant rainbow light of liberty and in an explosion of majesty your dreams will take flight on wings of hope, soaring into the eternal possibilities of your sublime magnificence.

The 20th Step

WHAT OF STEWARDSHIP?

I love the Earth and try to do my part to help keep it healthy like recycling and supporting worthy environmental causes. Yet, I know I could do more and there are billions of people who do almost nothing. What legacy are we leaving for our posterity? And I know stewardship is more than ecology. How can I best act as a good steward?

And my soul took flight and returned with an answer...

Your life is a shimmering treasure; a priceless gift beyond measure, for it not only gives you the wonders of living but also the opportunity to grow and expand from your varied experiences, ending your long journey far greater and more ennobled than you began. To pass through your sojourn you have been given a most marvelous planet to live upon, containing an abundance of everything you need to create comfort, health and longevity. You have been blessed with dutiful guardians who were ever diligent to care for you when you were too young to care for yourself and faithfully provided you the security and opportunity to develop your magnificent mind and body. You have further been gifted with the opportunity to gain tremendous depth and wisdom from your rich experiences and interactions with caring teachers, wise friends and helpful associates. Thus endowed with such a bounteous largesse, can you do anything less than be a good steward and preserve the remarkable inheritance that has been passed on to you, enriching and enlarging upon it that you may gratefully bestow a grander world to your posterity?

In the trackless immensity of space there are countless billions of galaxies. Within each unfathomable galaxy there can be many billions of suns, an infinitesimally small number of which twinkle as stars in your night sky. Orbiting around many of the suns are planets as innumerable in sum as the countless sands of the seashore. The small solar system of your yellow sun and the nine planets it sustains in orbit with its gravity, are a mere dust speck in the vast breadth of your single galaxy. Yet the third planet on which you dwell, the one called Earth, is a scintillating jewel in the vastness of the infinite universe; a loving matriarch who gives exhilarating life to all. In shameful ignorance is she profaned even as she continues to reward all with an extraordinary Eden to which none can compare.

Earth is a sun-kissed garden of lush green foliage and warm, sparkling, blue seas, covered from pole to pole with a teeming variety of life and vitality. Before you were nurtured in your mother's comforting womb, the Earth manifested the preeminent sanctuary of warmth, light, water and abundant food where all life could be conceived and thrive. Across its shining blue sphere, from environments hot to cold, wet to dry and night to day, your sacred planet is the hallowed nursery of all resident life that has ever been, all that is and all that will ever be. As a loving and devoted child, faithfully care for your Mother Earth even as she has always selflessly and abundantly cared for you.

You are energetically connected to all life; from your fellow beings of every color to a single blade of green grass, glistening with dew in the sunlight; for all have been nourished and owe their existence to the same loving mother Earth. All pulse with the same bioelectric energy swirling within the trillions of atoms which hold their form. All drink from the same everlasting water that first falls as rain upon the ground. All relish the same shimmering sun that spreads warmth and light across the world and the same spectral Moon that lights the night with ghostly beams. Through the food chain all are connected, as one life sustains another and all life forms exist only because your loving planet provides a sacred sanctuary, a tiny, warm, bubble of life within the sterile, frigid vacuum of space. The Earth benefits and enriches all life that dwells upon her; can you not do the same with all those whose lives you touch and, in greater measure still, reciprocate with love and consideration to the benevolent mother Earth who cherishes you and all your teeming kindred?

Greet each morning with a soft smile on your face, buoyant joy in your heart and lively gusto in your step, for another miracle day of life has dawned.

The good steward cultivates the garden of life in which they dwell that a plentiful harvest might ensue, overflowing with bounty for all. And how do you cultivate your garden into beautiful profusion? As you have received, so shall you give in greater measure that joy may dance with exuberance upon your life and your harvest may be multiplied with wonder and beneficence.

Be solicitous to those who cared and watched over you in your inquisitive youth, for by the dripping sweat of their brow and the selfless sacrifice of their time, they provided you with the opportunity to live your life and find your beckoning destiny.

Be a good and conscientious teacher to those who look to you for guidance, for you did not absorb your knowledge from the ethers, but only through the patience and diligence of others to your education.

Cherish and protect the sacred Earth and all of the life that dwells upon it, for by its bounty you are sustained each day and by your essential efforts the fragile cradle of life is preserved in health and vitality to provide in abundance for trusting generations unborn.

Love abundantly, for many others have first loved you and each wave of love you send out tenderly awashes you in return.

Give generously, for much has been given to you. Your dependable foundations of opportunity and success were laid by others who prepared and showed you the way. Some shared your life, some gave their lives and others are known only by the guiding words and inspiring works they left behind.

Always cherish the good fortune of your amazing life. You have the opportunity to reciprocate in thankfulness by fulfilling the full measure of your dazzling potential and giving the world your best. Anything less is unworthy of you and squanders the precious sacrifices made by many that you might gaze from a gleaming mountaintop upon a new and marvelous world.

The 21st Step

WHAT OF FAITH?

What does faith have to do with daily life? Are there common threads of faith and goodness that can bring people together instead of separating them? What is the role of religion? What is the essence of faith?

And my soul took flight and returned with an answer...

Faith is the fresh scent of blossoming flowers in the warm spring air, abiding in the cold, desolate depths of winter. It is the welcoming songs of awakening birds before the break of dawn and fields of tall corn waving in sunny, summer breezes as the farmer seeds the barren, fresh tilled Earth on a cold day in early spring. It is the trusting serenity of a child that all will be well, the continuing sacrifices of a parent for the visions of tomorrow and an expectant gaze for the refulgent coalesce of a rainbow through the misty veil of showers.

Faith is not a rare treasure found by just a chosen few; it is a divine force of the universe, permeating all things, the very breath of expectation upon which every action in life is taken. By faith, you rise in the morning to labor at your livelihood, with trust that you will be paid for your efforts. By faith, you marry your sweetheart with rising hope that your devoted love will see you safely through all the tempestuous trials of your journey together. By faith, you savor a tasty variety of food each day, believing you are giving your hungry body the necessary nourishment to sustain your life. Even the spiritually barren are upheld by lingering faith in every breath and action, for its ever abiding golden light intricately weaves scintillating threads of hope and motivation throughout the miraculous tapestry of life.

Throbbing faith of the loving heart lifts to heights sublime even as the bold faith of the nimble mind carries across chasms where frail hearts flutter. Yet the heart and mind are not disconnected acquaintances but intimately entwined friends through which faith beckons and motivates. Faith welling from the heart, and grounded in reason, flows and expands unconstrained through every fiber of the body. Like electricity, though mysteriously unseen and unfathomable, it manifests miraculous wonders, both diminutive and illustrious, as it lights and powers the bustling world. By evidence of what it has done, we have reliance in what it can do, even those things which we have never seen. Not simple undiscerning emotional belief without measured thought, but unhesitating trust of mind and heart confidently rising from firm foundations of past faith fulfilled, forged in the furnace of enduring truth, layer upon layer.

Yet, if a man has faith that he can successfully climb to the top of the towering mountain, but never leaves his doorstep, his faith is as the taste of a weak tea; a teasing hint of flavor, but without fulfillment or savor. Only when inner faith is married to resolute action and the journey up the soaring peak begun, can the delicious fruits of expanding faith be manifested and the lofty pinnacle of the peak be won.

Beware also of blind faith, reverberating nobly in the bosom but with emptiness in the head, for it can lead to perilous falls into cavernous pits. Verily, a faith that cannot endure honest scrutiny can exist only in a very narrow world; a fanaticism of the unknowing, leading the ignorant, into the non-existent.

Beyond the endless cavalcade of simple faith-based daily actions, spiritual faith exists on a higher peak in a loftier realm. From majestic heights of hope, a river of serenity flows through the human soul, softly humbling the heart, banishing pride and connecting contrite seekers of illumination to a divine reservoir within. It washes the aching heart with healing water that cleanses all pain and invigorates all hope. Though sometimes lost in the rush and trials of life, the tingling inner longing of unfulfilled spirituality forever beckons the resonating soul to reunite with its essence; to be lifted from the finite and mundane to the infinite and divine. It is a restless longing lingering in persistent quiet until fulfilled, for it is the life-giving sun searching for the sky and the stars of inspiration for the heavens.

Though religion may teach faith, it cannot hold it or define it, for it is a dynamic force that flows with a unique spiritual resonance through each individual. Although your spiritual faith may at times be an empty cup, it is one always beckoning to be filled, for in the purity of its depths are the luminous heights of your possibilities.

Remember, too, it is given to each person to drink from the spiritual cup of their choosing. Respect the chalice from which others choose to quench their thirst. Though you might choose another, each is drawn to the spiritual ambrosia that is most delicious and fulfilling to them at the time.

Faith, in the greater possibilities of life and eternity, begets a soaring personal spirituality that surmounts the fiery tribulations of life, affirming that there is more than the shell of your tenuous body, and endless time beyond the span of your days. Thus renews the eternal sojourn of the spirit. For what is spirituality but a noble, inner quest to commune with the sparkling divinity in all that is, to create a sweet, personal resonance with the timelessness of tomorrow that it may ever light the path of life today?

.

The 22nd Step

LOVE YOURSELF

And my soul took flight and returned with an answer...

1. Love yourself enough to **love yourself**; for your capacity to give love to others is only as great as your willingness to cede it to yourself.

2. Love yourself enough to **use common sense**; for a momentary thoughtless choice can bring a lifetime of grief, even as well considered actions can grant you a lifetime of peace and happiness.

3. Love yourself enough to **be true to yourself**; that you may always be guided to paths that will expand and delight you.

4. Love yourself enough to **have faith**; for it is the power by which you may accomplish all things.

5. Love yourself enough to **be honest with yourself**; that you may have a firm foundation to achieve your dreams.

6. Love yourself enough to **develop and use your mind**; for knowledge is freedom.

7. Love yourself enough to **hold optimism within your heart and thoughts**; for it lessens the sting of every trial and lays the foundation to vanquish every obstacle.

8. Love yourself enough to **be flexible and open to change**; for it is the only certain thing in life and to attempt to deny it is

to stagnate.

9. Love yourself enough to **play with laughter and spontaneit**y; that your inner child of yesteryear may ever live on, lighting your present with joy and smiles.

10. Love yourself enough to **work**; for in a worthy endeavor, by the sweat of your brow and the ingenuity of your mind, you create the future and sustain the present.

11. Love yourself enough to **ask for help when you need it and render it when you are asked**; for in asking, you edify those who selflessly render aid, and in assisting, you pass on a reciprocal energy that ripples into many lives.

12. Love yourself enough to **forgive and forget**; that you may release yourself to live anew.

13. Love yourself enough to **be a good steward**; for all that sustains your life is a gift of the Earth and the world you leave your children, for better or worse, is in your hands.

14. Love yourself enough to **stand back when pushed to the brink**; for there never was a heated moment that was not regretted, nor a cooler one that didn't offer a better choice.

15. Love yourself enough to **have a vision for the future**; for without it there is only existence and with it there is hope and inspiration.

16. Love yourself enough to **have passion**; for it enlivens you with positive energy and a natural euphoric fulfillment.

17. Love yourself enough to **be gently quiet**; that you may hear the wisdom of others, see the beauty that surrounds you and have time to reflect upon the gems of your journey.

18. Love yourself enough to **be daring**; for only those willing to venture beyond the shore can discover new worlds.

19. Love yourself enough to **laugh, especially at yourself**: for it eases the pains of life and helps to keep molehills from becoming mountains.

20. Love yourself enough to **treat your body like a temple**

inside and out; that it may bless you with physical health and mental clarity, adorn you in gracious beauty and give you the boundless energy and fortuitous longevity to experience life to the fullest.

21. Love yourself enough to **begin every venture with a positive attitude**; for the hills to climb will appear smaller and the victor's peak will arrive quicker.

22. Love yourself enough to **avoid dwelling in the past**; for when you look too long back at yesterday you miss all the wondrous joys abounding around you today.

23. Love yourself enough to **find a positive in every negative**; for all of life is a school and every experience a lesson.

24. Love yourself enough to **live up to your highest vision**; for when you expect great things, you lay the foundation to build your tower to the sky.

25. Love yourself enough to **give additional effort**; for those willing to run an extra mile will wear the winner's crown.

26. Love yourself enough to **do a good deed every day**; for the smallest kindness to others is greater than the most illustrious of intentions.

27. Love yourself enough to **help others reach their dreams**; for the lift you give them raises you as well and in their fulfillment you find your own.

28. Love yourself enough to **accept that you are not perfect**; and that your best effort is a worthy victory.

29. Love yourself enough to **discover and connect to your inner core**; for only when you see yourself as you really are can you find the path that leads to who you can be.

30. Love yourself enough to **refuse to falter because of failures**; for your unfulfilled victories wait for you still, if you will but finish the race.

31. Love yourself enough to have the **moral courage to speak up when injustices are committed against others**; for in silence

you are an accomplice and in voice justice resounds far beyond the space in which you stand.

32. Love yourself enough to **cultivate balance in your essence**; that you may stand steady when the path is tumultuous and be able to safely pass over the yawing pitfalls of life.

33. Love yourself enough to **embrace challenges as a regular part of life**; for only when you are tested do you gain the strength to grow and expand.

34. Love yourself enough to **dream**; for only upon their sparkling wings can you soar above the clutter and see the magnificence that awaits you in the distance.

35. Love yourself enough to **admire the beauty and grandeur of nature**; for its quiet wonder sings a soothing song of peace and an enlivening melody of hope.

36. Love yourself enough to **weep**; for every tear that falls purges your heart of poison and when you lift your head you can see the brilliant, new sun of promise through the mist.

37. Love yourself enough to give **respect and courtesy to others**; for it is the basic foundation of all beneficial, reciprocal relationships.

38. Love yourself enough to **fulfill your responsibilities**; for the trust you gain from others is more precious than gold and you lay the enduring foundation for your own self-worth.

39. Love yourself enough to be s**piritually and energetically connected to all that exists**; for when you feel the pulse of oneness in all things, it is easy to love the Earth and everyone upon it, for you are only cherishing an essential part of yourself.

40. Love yourself enough to **keep an open mind**; for a closed vessel will stagnate in its own waste and in openness you will find answers to riddles you could not fathom.

41. Love yourself enough to **avoid criticizing others**; for you only demean yourself and a kind word instead will lift you both to a higher plateau.

42. Love yourself enough to **repent and ask forgiveness**; for to ere is inescapable and hiding the wrong will only be self-destructive. The forgiveness you merit will become a hallowed remembrance, allowing forgiveness of others when they have trespassed against you.

43. Love yourself enough to **love and be loved**; for it taps an emotional well that enlivens every fiber of your being and fulfills every longing of your heart.

44. Love yourself enough to **reflect and be introspective**; for only when you gaze deeply into the labyrinth of your heart and mind can you realistically understand your strengths and weaknesses, assess how far you have come, crystallize where you want to go and formulate the best way to get there.

45. Love yourself enough to **keep an open heart**; for to lock your emotional door is to imprison yourself and turn away from the sweetness of happiness and joy.

46. Love yourself enough to **focus**; for your efforts are magnified and the fires of success burn bright only with an undistracted beam of effort that holds unwaveringly to your goal.

47. Love yourself enough to **be friendly**; for it is an elixir that sweetens the sourest dispositions, endearing friends and disarming adversaries.

48. Love yourself enough to **gain knowledge**; for ignorance is a path to mediocrity while knowledge is the portal to making dreams come true.

49. Love yourself enough to **refuse to gossip**; for to speak ill of another behind their back while smiling courteously in their presence, is to dig a two-faced morass of pettiness into which you to will one day fall without pity.

50. Love yourself enough to be **artistically creative**; for it is an ability that dwells within everyone and nurturing it into fullness unleashes a host of other talents that would have otherwise lain unknown and undiscovered.

51. Love yourself enough to **slow down and relax**; for what is the purpose of toil if you never have time to enjoy life?

52. Love yourself enough to show **sincere appreciation**; for your kind words are a balm of joy and an affirmation of pride that brings smiles and light even on the darkest day.

53. Love yourself enough to **meditate**; for it stills your restless mind and calms your anxious heart, bringing you revitalized into a new day.

54. Love yourself enough to be **kind to animals**; for the timber of your character is bared in its true form by the demonstrations of how you treat those who are defenseless before you.

55. Love yourself enough to **honor uplifting traditions**; for they are the memories of tomorrow, bequeathed in yesterday and savored today.

56. Love yourself enough to **be engaged in charitable causes**; for in selfless service to others you earn a measure of humility and a reward of gratitude greater than any monetary compensation.

57. Love yourself enough to **persevere in your endeavors**; for success waits around the next bend for the stalwart champions who stay the course till the end.

58. Love yourself enough to **get a good night's sleep**; for in your long, restful slumber you lay the foundation for a morrow that is fresher and fuller.

59. Love yourself enough to **give of your time**; for it is a most precious finite treasure, a true gift, valued greatly by all with whom you share it.

60. Love yourself enough to **do your best today**; for nothing less is worthy of you. Tomorrow is the day reserved for that which may never be, while today's victory merely awaits your resolve.

61. Love yourself enough to **cultivate a good disposition**; for you are planting a garden of civility that will spread sunshine and joy to all who partake of your company.

62. Love yourself enough to **be a peace maker**; for within an

aura of respectful, reasoned, resolve, the damaging animosity of antagonists can be turned into a boon of mutual reward.

63. Love yourself enough to **speak and act positively**; for your living sunshine brightens any day and sets in motion the energies necessary to accomplish all your desires.

64. Love yourself enough to **hold serenity at the center of your being**; for when the waters of peace wash over your soul the fiery darts of life fizzle into harmless wisps of insignificance that cannot pierce you.

65. Love yourself enough to **avoid blaming others for your problems**; for deflecting cause to another merely delays correcting the flaws within yourself that allowed the problem to manifest.

66. Love yourself enough to **never hate others**; for every minute wasted in hatred is a minute lost from your life, a frittering away of time to have joy in exchange for a wrenching pit of perpetual emptiness.

67. Love yourself enough to **let go of guilt**; for everyone makes mistakes. Make amends to those wronged and within yourself, then go forward with a good heart, in forgiveness and forgetfulness, or the recriminations from the past will always present a ghostly door barring your entry to the future.

68. Love yourself enough to **have relationships with equal energy exchanges**; for as the bee takes pollen from the flower which is in turn reproduced because of the bee, so too the health of your self-esteem calls for reciprocation in some form of equal measure to those who benefit you and avoidance of those who do not give you the same consideration.

69. Love yourself enough to **abandon anger residing within you**; for the fire of rage you stoke will burn you the most.

70. Love yourself enough to **love life even with all its challenges and imperfections**; for it gives you the opportunity to learn and grow, to love and find happiness and to leave the

world better than you found it.

71. Love yourself enough to **be refreshed by new things**; for the lake of your life will stagnate and dry up unless it is continually invigorated by the stimulating inflow of fresh experiences and new knowledge.

72. Love yourself enough to **help others with their grief**; for the empathy and sympathy you give is a balm of solace that enriches you in the giving and opens you to receiving a gift that you too will someday need.

73. Love yourself enough to **rid your life of stress**; for it is a merciless foe that chips away at your vitality, robbing you of precious years of life and many moments of happiness.

74. Love yourself enough to **love and honor nature in all of its forms**; for it is a refuge of serenity, bestowing light, warmth, beauty and sustenance; asking only that you faithfully keep it healthy and vibrant that it may ever be there to provide refreshing abundance for you and your posterity.

75. Love yourself enough to **simplify your life**; for with every superfluous layer you strip away you add resounding depth and luster.

76. Love yourself enough to **flow to your own rhythm**, for you will be more fulfilled in an hour paced by your own inner pulse, than you will ever be trying to abide by someone else's cadence.

77. Love yourself enough to **be a good example**; for by your actions many with whom you associate are also judged, and by the uprightness of your deeds you open the door to others who may be seeking the light.

78. Love yourself enough to **have no place for worry in your heart or mind**; for during the time wasted in concern about circumstances that may never be, things that are tangible and in your hand may become neglected and lost.

79. Love yourself enough to **tell the truth**; for lies come back

to bite you; they dampen your inner light with every one you tell, while your honesty is a firm foundation upon which friends and associates will confidently trust.

80. Love yourself enough to **refrain from judging others**; for to mete out criticism by thought or action, simply because another's personal choices in life are different than yours, is to allow the pettiest of character traits to hold sway over the noblest.

81. Love yourself enough to **create a sacred space in or near your home**; for you will find restful tranquility and lucid answers in a hallowed sanctuary where you can forget the world and commune in thoughtfulness with your higher self and the divine energies of the universe that smile upon you.

82. Love yourself enough to **communicate thoughtfully and clearly**; for both the written and spoken word have the power to burn or heal, anger or motivate, crush or uplift.

83. Love yourself enough to **be enthusiastic**; for it is the spark that creates bonfires of success, impels others to greater efforts and snatches victory from defeat.

84. Love yourself enough to **be sincerely interested in other people**; for to learn all they have to teach you from their lives, you must take the time to earnestly listen to their experiences and wisdom.

85. Love yourself enough to **create a legacy that will outlast you**; that your stature may grow with your foresight and the good light of your life may continue to spread sunshine upon the world, enriching the lives of generations to come.

86. Love yourself enough to **honor your truth and walk your talk**; for your noble words and beliefs are as worthless as dust upon the desert wind unless you give them substance and meaning by living your ideals everyday.

87. Love yourself enough to **seek out and find God**, for your immutable connection to something greater will always beckon and you will only find the fullness you seek once you heed the

call.

88. Love yourself enough to **pay attention to the longings of your spirit**; for the bridge to happiness that spans the chasm of life's irrelevance can only be discovered when you listen to your inner yearnings calling you to your destiny.

EMBROSEWYN'S BOOKS

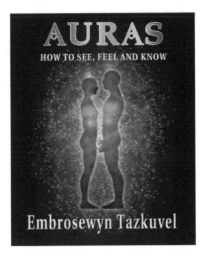

AURAS

How To See, Feel And Know

Auras: *How to See, Feel & Know*, is like three books in one!

- It's an entertaining read as Embrosewyn recalls his early childhood and high school experiences seeing auras, and the often humorous reactions by everyone from his mother to his friends when he told them what he saw.
- It is also a complete training manual to help you quickly be able to see Auras in vibrant color. It includes 17 eye exercises and dozens of Full Color pictures, enabling anyone with vision in both eyes to begin seeing vividly colored auras around any person. The secret is in retraining the focusing parts of your eyes to see things that have always been there, but you have never been able to see before. Auras: How to See, Feel & Know, includes all the power techniques, tools and Full Color eye exercises from Embrosewyn's popular workshops.

• Additionally, there is a fascinating chapter on body language. Embrosewyn teaches in his workshops to not just rely on your interpretation of the aura alone, but to confirm it with another indicator such as body language. Auras: How to See, Feel & Know goes in depth with thorough explanations and great pictures to show you all the common body language indicators used to confirm what someone's aura is showing you.

For those who already have experience seeing auras, the deeper auric layers and subtle auric nuances and the special ways to focus your eyes to see them, are explained in detail, with accompanying Full Color pictures to show you how the deeper layers and auric aberrations appear.

Secret Earth Series

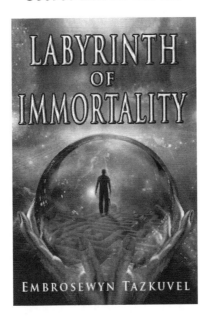

LABYRINTH OF IMMORTALITY
BOOK 1

Could it be possible that there is a man alive on the Earth today that has been here for two thousand years? How has he lived so long? And why? What secrets does he know? Can his knowledge save the Earth or is it doomed?

Continuing the epic historical saga begun in the *Oracles of Celestine Light*, but in a novel form, Labyrinth of Immortality is the first book of the new *Secret Earth series* chronicling the life and adventures of Lazarus of Bethany and his powerful and mysterious sister Miriam of Magdala, known by the world today as Mary Magdalene. But she is soooo much more than the world knows or imagines!

~Coming Soon~
ANGEL OF THE COVENANT

Book 2

MYSTIQUE OF DESTINY
Book 3

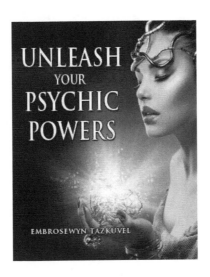

UNLEASH YOUR PSYCHIC POWERS

A comprehensive guidebook for all levels of practitioners of the psychic and paranormal arts. Each one of the twenty supernatural abilities presented, including Clairvoyance, Animal Whispering, Lucid Dreaming, Precognition, Astral Projection, Channeling, Telekinesis and Telepathy, include easy-to-follow, step-by-step instructions on how you can unleash the full potential of these potent powers in your own life. Spiced with personal stories of Embrosewyn's five decades of experience discovering, developing and using psychic and paranormal talents. Paranormal abilities have saved Embrosewyn's life and the lives of his family members on multiple occasions. Learning to fully develop your own supernatural talents may come in just as handy one day.

PSYCHIC SELF DEFENSE

Have you ever felt a negative energy come over you for no apparent reason when you are near someone or around certain places? Psychic Self Defense details 17 common psychic threats, with exact, effective counter measures including many real life examples from Embrosewyn's 5 decades of personal experiences with the paranormal, devising what works and what doesn't from hard won trial and error.

Both the neophyte and the experienced will find a wealth of specific how-to methods to counter all forms of psychic attacks: from projections of negative thoughts from other people, to black magic curses, to hauntings by disembodied spirits, to energy sucking vampires, or attacks by demons.

Psychic Self Defense should be in the library of every psychic and serious student of the paranormal, and absolutely read by every medium, channeler, or person who makes any contact with forces, entities, or beings from the world beyond.

Psychic Self Defense is also available as an AUDIO BOOK.

LOVE YOURSELF
The Secret Key to Transforming Your Life

Loving yourself is all about energy. As humans we devote a great deal of our energy through our time, thoughts and emotions to love. We read about it, watch movies and shows about it, dream about it, hope for it to bless our lives, feel like something critically important is lacking when it doesn't, and at the very least keep a sharp eye out for it when its missing.

Too often we look to someone else to fulfill our love and crash and burn when relationships end, or fail to live up to our fantasies of what we thought they should be. Helping those situations to never occur begins with loving yourself first. It is a precious gift from you to you. An incredibly powerful energy that not only enhances your ability to give love more fully to others, but also creates a positive energy of expanding reverberation that brings more love, friendship and appreciation to you from all directions. It is the inner light that illuminates your life empowering you to create the kind of life you desire and dream. Helping you along the way, you'll find a gift inside of 88 reasons to love yourself.

Special Bonus: Love Yourself is ALSO AVAILABLE AS AN AUDIO BOOK! This allows you to listen and read at the same time!

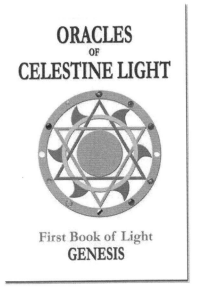

ORACLES
OF
CELESTINE LIGHT

First Book of Light
GENESIS

GENESIS
FIRST BOOK OF LIGHT

The first book of light in the Oracles of Celestine Light trilogy. Ancient knowledge uncovered by a modern prophet, Genesis reveals how the universe and the Earth were actually created and how the Earth was first peopled with modern humans. The truth may shock you but it will make infinitely more sense than the commonly accepted scriptural stories!

Genesis also reveals the true story of Noah and the Ark (hint: it has nothing to do with a boat!).

Also revealed in Genesis is the detailed, event-filled true story of the rise and destruction of what is known today as Atlantis. Plus, the true location where the ruins of this fabulous city can be found today, along with the library of knowledge preserved for future generations!

Genesis also gives details about the history of giants on the planet in ancient times and the significant part advanced alien races played in the rise of civilizations.

The last chapter reaches through time to give you a moving ancient sermon on life and happiness that resonates as strongly today as it did thousands of years ago.

ORACLES
OF
CELESTINE LIGHT

Second Book of Light
NEXUS

NEXUS
SECOND BOOK OF LIGHT

Nexus, The Second Book of Celestine Light, contains 44 chapters. It is a chronological record taking place about 2,000 years ago that begins with the birth of Yeshua of Nazareth, known to most people in the world today as Jesus. It recounts his previously unknown life and teachings up until the time his ministry begins in his late twenties.

As he was growing up, Yeshua had many influential teachers from lands near and far, and the significant interplay he had with them is faithfully recorded.

Nexus also reveals the full story of the close kinship and experiences shared by Yeshua and his cousin Yochanan the Baptizer, known today as John the Baptist.

Yeshua was married at the age of 18 to Miriam of Magdala and from that moment she became his constant companion and grew into a woman of great spiritual power and authority in her own right. Much of Nexus reveals the details of their life together, including the birth of their two children and the family's travels and adventures while living in Egypt for some years.

Everyone is familiar with the Ten Commandments, but in Nexus we discover there were originally twelve commandments and all of these have significant differences and go into more detail than the ten commonly known.

Many of the events recounted in Nexus are found in no other book on Earth. These include several profound and moving sermons missing from modern religious texts. For both, Christians and non-Christians, the lost teachings of Yeshua unveiled in Nexus provide a blueprint for a happy life, with wise counsel that will guide you to greater fulfillment on whatever path you choose.

ORACLES
OF
CELESTINE LIGHT

Third Book of Light
VIVUS

VIVUS
THIRD BOOK OF LIGHT

Vivus, The Third Book of Celestine Light, is a monumental book containing 100 chapters detailing the life and teachings of Yeshua of Nazareth during the time corresponding to the extremely limited account in the Christian New Testament.

Vivus not only includes many sermons and descriptions of profound miracles not found in other books, but also fills in many lost details to the sermons, miracles and accounts that are mentioned in other documents.

In Vivus we get to witness the evolution of both Yeshua and Miriam as they both come to a full understanding of who they are and the great power that comes with that knowledge to both of them.

Yeshua calls twelve Apostles or 'special witnesses' in Vivus, and Miriam, as one of the twelve, becomes the 'Apostle to the Apostles.'

Throughout much of the latter half of Vivus Yeshua is

continually teaching his Apostles the secrets and mysteries of the Celestine Light by which all things are possible. In the course of this we learn that the Earth is only one of countless Earths and Yeshua explains many paranormal activities and abilities, and how these can be utilized and controlled by the Adepts of the Children of Light.

Like Nexus, the chapters of Vivus are chronological and are best read one after the other, as there are often essential foundations laid in earlier chapters that help you to better understand the events in later chapters.

Psychic Awakening Series

CLAIRVOYANCE
BOOK 1

Would it be helpful to you if you could gain hidden knowledge about a person, place, thing, event, or concept, not by any of your five physical senses, but with visions and "knowing?" *Clairvoyance* takes you on a quest of self-discovery and empowerment, helping you unlock this potent ability in your life. It includes riveting personal stories from Embrosewyn's six decades of psychic and paranormal adventures, plus fascinating accounts of others as they discovered and cultivated their supernatural abilities.

Clearly written, step-by-step practice exercises will help you to expand and benefit from your own clairvoyant abilities. This can make a HUGE improvement in your relationships, career and creativity. As Embrosewyn has proven from over twenty years helping thousands of students to find and develop their psychic and paranormal abilities, EVERYONE, has one or more supernatural gifts. *Clairvoyance* will help you discover and unleash yours!

Psychic Awakening Series
Book 2

TELEKINESIS

EMBROSEWYN TAZKUVEL

TELEKINESIS
BOOK 2

Telekinesis, also known as psychokinesis, is the ability to move or influence the properties of objects without physical contact. Typically it is ascribed as a power of the mind. But as Embrosewyn explains, based upon his 5 decades of personal experience, the actual physical force that moves and influences objects emanates from a person's auric field. It initiates with a mental thought, but the secret to the power is in your aura!

This book is filled with proven, exercises and training techniques to help you unlock this formidable paranormal ability. Spiced with accounts of real-life experiences by both Embrosewyn and others, you'll be entertained while you learn. But along the way you will begin to unleash the potent power of *Telekinesis* in your own life!

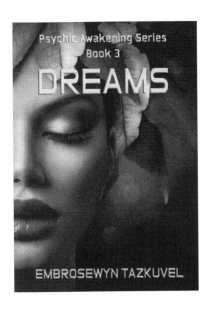

DREAMS
BOOK 3

In **Dreams**, renowned psychic/paranormal practitioner Embrosewyn Tazkuvel reveals some of his personal experiences with the transformational effect of dreams, while sharing time-tested techniques and insights that will help you unlock the power of your own night travels.

An expanded section on Lucid Dreaming gives you proven methods to induce and expand your innate ability to control your dreams. It explores the astonishing hidden world of your dream state that can reveal higher knowledge, greatly boost your creativity, improve your memory, and help you solve vexing problems of everyday life that previously seemed to have no solution.

Detailing the nine types of dreams will help you to understand which dreams are irrelevant and which you should pay close attention to, especially when they reoccur. You'll gain insight into how to interpret the various types of dreams to understand which are warnings of caution, and which are gems of inspiration that can change your life from the moment you awaken and begin to act upon that which you dreamed.

Dreaming while you sleep is a part of your daily life and cumulatively it accounts for dozens of years of your total life. It is a valuable time of far more than just rest. Become the master of your dreams and your entire life can become more than you ever imagined possible. Your dreams are the secret key to your future.

A Note From Embrosewyn About Your Soul Name

As many people who have read my books or attended my seminars over the years are aware, one of the things I use my psychic gifts for is to discover a person's Soul Name. Knowing this name and the meaning and powers of the sounds has proven to be transformational in the lives of some people. It has always been a great privilege for me to be asked to find a Soul Name for someone. But as my books have become more popular and numerous over the years, with new titles actively in the works in both the *Secret Earth series* and the *Awakening Psychic series*, plus sequels to popular stand alone books such as *Auras*, I have less and less time available to discover a Soul Name for someone when they request it. Doing so requires up to 2 hours of uninterrupted meditation time, which is a fairly great challenge for me to find these days.

With these time constraints in mind, I have been forced to raise the price to limit the requests to people who are truly ready to know their Soul Name and embrace their inherent powers and abilities. Some people have assumed this was done to make more money. Just the opposite is the case. The higher price for my time dissuades most people from asking for their Soul Name. For every ten requests I used to receive, I now get one. So the net to my income is much less, not more. But for me, time is most precious and this is the way it must be if I am to accomplish all I need to in this life. I do hope everyone will understand. If you would like to know more about Soul Names please visit this site, *www.mysoulname.com.*

Namaste,

Embrosewyn

24458069R00078

Made in the USA
Middletown, DE
24 September 2015